William Hughes, John Dennys

The Secrets of Angling Teaching the Choicest Tools, Baits and Seasons...

Vol. I

William Hughes, John Dennys

The Secrets of Angling Teaching the Choicest Tools, Baits and Seasons...
Vol. I

ISBN/EAN: 9783337165840

Printed in Europe, USA, Canada, Australia, Japan

Cover: Foto ©Lupo / pixelio.de

More available books at **www.hansebooks.com**

Bibliotheca Curiosa.

THE
Secrets of Angling:

TEACHING
THE CHOICEST TOOLS, BAITS, AND SEASONS,
FOR THE TAKING OF ANY FISH
IN
POND OR RIVER,

Practised and familiarly opened in three Books,

BY
J. D., Esquire.

EDITED BY "PISCATOR."

IN TWO VOLUMES.

Vol. I.

PRIVATELY PRINTED, EDINBURGH.

1885.

Secrets of Angling.

Bibliotheca Curiosa.

THE
Secrets of Angling:

TEACHING
THE CHOICEST TOOLS, BAITS,
AND SEASONS,
FOR THE TAKING OF ANY FISH
IN
POND OR RIVER,
Practised and familiarly opened
in three Books,

BY

J. D., Esquire,

EDITED BY "PISCATOR."

IN TWO VOLUMES.
Vol. I.

PRIVATELY PRINTED, EDINBURGH.

1885.

Introduction.

"THERE appears to be no poetical treatise on the gentle craft of earlier date than Dennys's "Secrets of Angling." Some think that these verses have never been surpassed by any other Angling poet. Beloe, in his "Anecdotes of Literature and Scarce Books," says:—"Perhaps there does not exist in the circle of English Literature a rarer book than this." It was first printed for Roger Jackson in 1613, under the title, "The Secrets of Angling: Teaching The Choicest Tools, Baits & Seasons, for the taking of any Fish in Pond or River: practised and familiarly opened in three Books. By J. D. Esquire." Whatever doubts may have existed about the name of the author are now removed by the discovery of the entry of the book in the Stationers' Register, wherein John Dennys is named as the author. But who this Dennys certainly was is still unsettled. There was a well-known Gloucestershire family of that name, and there was a member of that family by name John,

son of Hugh Dennys by Katherine Tyre: he died
and was buried at Pucklechurch, in 1609. Roger
Jackson, for whom the first edition of 1613 was
printed, says, in his dedicatory letter, that the
poem was sent to him to be printed after (and may
it not be presumed shortly?) the death of the
author. John Dennys, just mentioned as son of
Hugh Dennys, is supposed to be the same person
as John Dennys, the author of the "Secrets of
Angling." "The Fisherman's Magazine," and
"Notes and Queries,"* contain much that is
interesting about the Dennys pedigree, and the
editions of the "Secrets of Angling." There are
four editions. Copies of the first edition are
extremely rare, so rare indeed that Mr. Arber in
his preface to the reprint† of it in the first volume
of the "English Garner" (London, 1877), says
only two copies of the first edition are known to
exist; the one is in the Bodleian and the other

---

* Only nineteen numbers of the "Fisherman's
Magazine," which consists of two volumes, were
published: the first number appeared in April, 1864,
the last in October, 1865. See especially Mr. Westwood's letters in the numbers of "Notes and Queries,"
30th November, 1867, 28th December, 1867, 31st
July, 1869 (this announces the discovery of the date
of the third edition, viz. 1650), and 28th August
1869.

† In this "reprint" the spelling is modernised, and
several alterations made in the original text.

Introduction

was in the collection of the late Mr. Henry Huth who lent his copy to Mr. Arber for the purpose of his reprint. The date of the second edition is conjectured to be about 1620, and in this edition the work is described as being augmented with many approved experiments. The editor was William Lauson, whose comments appear in the form of notes to this edition. The poem is divided into three books, which treat very fully of everything appertaining to the sport: it is in the first book that "The Antiquity of Angling" is noticed, while some of the verses of the third are devoted to "the twelve virtues and qualities which ought to be in every Angler." Izaak Walton says there can be no doubt "but that Angling is an art, and an art worth your learning: the question is rather whether you be capable of learning it. For angling is somewhat like poetry, men are to be born so."—["Complete Angler," pt. i., cap. 1.] Dennys was both poet and angler born; his verses are admired and bespeak a natural love of the art whose praises he so quaintly sings. The treatise on angling contained in "The Pleasures of Princes; or, Good Men's Recreations" (4to., London, 1614, and other editions), is said to have been rendered into prose from Dennys's "Secrets of Angling."

The qualications necessary for an angler, according to this curious old book, are very numerous. "A skilful Angler," it is said, "ought to bee a generall scholler, and seene in all the Liberall Sciences; as a Grammarian" he ought "to know how either to Write or Discourse of his Art in true and fitting termes, either without affectation or rudenes. He should have sweetness of speech . . . . strength of arguments . . . . knowledge in the Sunne, Moone, and Starres . . . . Hee should bee a good knower of Countries. . . . Hee should have knowledge in proportions of all sorts, whether Circular, Square, or Diametricall. . . . He must also have the perfect Art of numbring. . . . Hee should not be unskilfull in Musick, that whensoever either melancholly, heavinesse of his thought, or the perturbations of his own fancies stirreth up sadnesse in him hee may remove the same with some godly Hymne or Antheme, of which David gives him ample examples." Hope, brotherly love, patience, and humility should all find place in his heart. "Then he must be strong and valient, neither to be amazed with Stormes nor affrighted with Thunder;" and there are many other qualities mentioned in "The whole Art of Angling" as being also necessary to the fisherman."[*]

The notes I have added are from a variety of sources. First, William Lawson's, distinguished by the initials, W. L. Then descriptions of fish

---

[*] Lambert's "Angling Literature of England," pp. 43-50.

as given in Salter's well-known Angler's guide; hints and "wrinkles" from Ephemera, Francis, and most modern writers on the gentle art, and lastly a few observations due to my own personal experience. I have not quoted Walton; his book is, of course, a household word with every brother of the angle.

"PISCATOR."

EDINBURGH,
   Oct. 12, 1885.

TO THE WORTHY, AND MY MVCH RESPECTED FRIEND, Mr. IOHN HARBORNE, of Tackley, in the Countie of Oxford, Esquire.

WORTHY Syr, this Poeme being sent vnto me to be printed after the death of the Author, who intended to haue done it in his life, but was preuented by death: I could not among my good friends, bethinke me of anyone to whom I might more fitly dedicate it (as well for the nature of the subiect in which you delight as to expresse my loue) than to your selfe. I finde it not onely sauouring of Art and Honesty, two things now strangers vnto many Authors, but also both pleasant and profitable; and being loath to see a thing of such value lye hidden in obscuritie, whilest matters of no moment pester the stales of euery Stationer; I therefore make bolde to publish it, for the benefit and delight of all, trusting that

THE DEDICATION.

I shall neither thereby disparage the Author, nor dislike them. I neede not, I think, Appollogise either the vse of the subiect, or for that it is reduced into the nature of a Poeme; for as touching the last (in that it is in verse) some count it by so much the more delightfull; and I holde it euery way as fit a subject for Poetry as Husbandry: and touching the first, if Hunting & Hawking haue beene thought worthy delights and Artes to be instructed in, I make no doubt but this Art of Angling is muche more worthy practise and approbation; for it is a sport euery way as pleasant, lesse chargeable, more profitable, and nothing so much subiect to choller or impatience as those are: you shall finde it more briefly, pleasantly, & more exactly performed, then any of this kinde heretofore. Therefore I referre you to the perusing thereof, and my selfe to your good opinion, which I tender as that holde most deere; euer remaining at

Your gentle Command,
R. I.

In dew praise of this Praise-worthy Skill and Worke.

IN skils that all doe seeke, but few doe finde,
   Both gaine and game; (like Sunne and Moone doe shine)
   Then th' Art of Fishing thus is of that kinde;
The Angler taketh both with Hooke and Line.
And as, with Lines, both these he takes; this takes,
With many a Line, well made, both Eares and Harts,
And, by this skill, the skill-lesse skill-full makes:
The Corpes whereof discected so he parts,
Vpon an humble Subiect neuer lay
More proude, yet plainer Lines, the plaine to leade,
This playner Art with pleasure to suruay,
To purchase it, with profit, by that Deed:
   Who thinke this skill's too low than, for the high
   This Angler reade, and they'll be tane thereby.*

Io. Dauies.

---

* One might be reading a bit of Browning!

THE CONTENTS.

The first Booke containeth these 3 heads

1. THE antiquitie of Angling, with the Art of Fishing, and of Fish in generall.

2. The lawfulnesse, pleasure, and profit thereof, with all Obiections, answered, against it.

3. To know the season, and times to prouide the Tooles, and how to choose the best, and the manner how to make them fit to take each seuerall Fish.

The second Booke, containeth

1. THE Anglers experience, how to v.e his Tooles and Baytes, to make profit by his game.

2. What Fish is not taken with Angle, and what is: and which is best for health.

3. In what Waters and Riuers to finde each Fish.

The thirde Booke containeth

1. THE 12 vertues and qualities which ought to be in euery Angler.

2. What weather, seasons, and times of the yeere is best and worst, and what houres of the day is best for sport.

3. To knowe each Fishes haunt, and the times to take them.

Also, an obscure secret, of an approued Bait, tending thereunto.

THE
Secrets of Angling.

The first Booke.

OF Angling, and the Art thereof I sing,
   What kinde of Tooles it doth behoue
      to haue,
   And with what pleasing bayt a man
      may bring
The Fish to bite within the watry waue.
A worke of thankes to such as in a thing
Of harmlesse pleasure, haue regard to saue
   Their dearest soules from sinne; and may intend
   Of pretious time, some part thereon to spend.

You Nymphs that in the Springs and Waters
   sweet,
Your dwelling haue, of euery Hill and Dale,
And oft amidst the Meadowes greene doe meet,
To sport and play, and heare the Nightingale;
And in the Riuers fresh doe wash your feet,
While Prognes sister* tels her wofull tale:
   Such ayde and power vnto my verses lend,
   As may suffice this little worke to end.

And thou sweet Boyd† that with thy watry sway,
Dost wash the cliffes of Deington and of Weeke;
And through their Rockes with crooked winding
   way,
Thy mother Auon runnest soft to seeke:
In whose fayre streames the speckled Trout doth
   play,
The Roche, the Dace, the Gudgin and the Bleeke,

---

* The swallow. According to Grecian fable, Progne was sister of Philomela, and wife of Tereus. Tereus having offered violence to Philomela, cut out her tongue that she might not expose him, and then told his wife that she was dead. The truth being discovered, Tereus would have slain both the sisters; but Philomela was changed into a nightingale and Progne into a swallow.
   As Progne or as Philomela mourns. . .
   That finds the nest by cruel hands despoiled,
   So Bradamant laments her absent knight.
         "*Orlando Furioso,*" bk. xxiii.
† The name of a brook.

Teach me the skill with slender Line and
  Hooke
To take each Fish of Riuer, Pond, and Brooke.

The time for prouiding the Angle Rods.

FIRST, when the Sunne beginneth to
    decline
  Southward his course, with his fayre
    Chariot bright,
  And passed hath of Heauen the middle
Line,
That makes of equall length both day and night:
And left behind his backe the dreadfull signe,
Of cruell Centaure,* slaine in drunken fight,
  When Beasts do mourne, and Birds forsake
    their song,
  Ahe euery Creature thinks the night too long.

And blustring *Boreas* with his chilling cold,
Vnclothed hath the Trees of Sommers greene;
And Woods and Groues are naked to behold,
Of Leaues and Branches now dispoyled cleane:

---

* The Thessalonian Centaurs were half horses, half men. Being invited to a marriage feast, they became intoxicated and assaulted the women. The Lapithæ took the part of the women and drove the Centaurs out of the country.

So that their fruitfull stocks they doe vnfold,
And lay abroad their of-spring to be seene;
  Where nature shewes her great increase of kinde
  To such as seeke their tender shutes to finde.

Then goe into some great Arcadian wood,
Where store of ancient Hazels doe abound;
And seeke amongst their springs and tender brood,
Such shutes as are the straightest, long and round:
And of them all (store vp what you think good)
But fairest choose, the smoothest and most sound;
  So that they doe not two yeares growth exceed,
  In shape and beautie like the Belgicke Reed.

These prune and clense of euery leafe and spray,
Yet leaue the tender top remaining still:*
Then home with thee goe beare them safe away,
But perish not the Riue and vtter Pill;†
And on some euen boarded floore them lay
Where they may dry and season at their fill:‡
  And place vpon their crooked parts some waight
  To presse them downe, and keepe them plaine and straight.

---

* Bathe them a little except the top, all in a furnace: they will be lighter and not top heavy; which is a great fault in a rod.—W. L.

† Rind and bark (peel).

‡ Tie them together at every bout, and they will keep one another straight.—W. L.

So shalt thou haue always in store the best,
And fittest Rods to serue thy turne aright;
For not the brittle Cane, nor all the rest,
I like so well, though it be long and light,
Since that the Fish are frighted with the least
Aspect of any glittering thing, or white:*
  Nor doth it by one halfe so well incline,†
  As both the plyant rod to saue the line.‡

---

* White or grey are likest the sky, and therefore of all colors offend the least.—W. L.

† Besides the fish discerns it, and is put away with the stiffness of the rod; whereas on the contrary the weak rod yields liberty to the fish without suspicion, to run away with the bait at his pleasure.—W. L.

‡ In bottom fishing the rod should not be less than 15 or 16 feet, and on the Lea, fishermen even use rods of 22 or 23 feet. They should be light, and white East India cane is the best material. In punt fishing 12 to 13 feet is the best size, and bamboo should be the wood employed. The Nottingham Anglers use a light and springy rod, more flexible than a punt rod, but less so than a fly rod. In spinning for Jack, the rod should be about 14 or 15 feet in length, and of solid wood, greenheart for preference. For Trout-fishing a single, or double-handed rod may be used. If the former, it should be twelve feet long, and not more than 13½ oz. in weight. It should be moderately pliable. If a double-rod is preferred, choose one 14½ feet long, the two lower joints being of bamboo, with a greenheart top. Many Anglers prefer Hickory rods, and perhaps for large fish they may be better up to the

To make the Line.

GOOD Hayre then get, so that it be
    not blacke;
Neither of Mare nor Gelding let it
    be;
Nor of the tyreling Iade that
beares the packe:
But of some lusty Horse or Courser free,
Whose bushie tayle vpon the ground doth tracke
Like blazing Comete that sometimes we see:
    From out the mid'st thereof the longest take
    At leysure best your Linkes and Lines to
        make.

Then twist them finely, as you thinke most
    meet,
By skill or practise easy to be found;

---

work, but they are somewhat heavier, and this tells in a long day's fishing. For Salmon, the rod should be from 16 to 17½ feet long, unless the Angler be exceptionally tall and strong, when he may use one of 20 or 21 feet. Greenheart and Hickory are the best woods, though Mr. Francis recommends Washaba, a new wood. The weight should be about 2½ lbs. for a rod of sixteen feet nine inches, and about 2 lbs. 13 oz. for a rod of nineteen and a half feet.

As doth Arachne* with her slender feet;†
Draw forth her little thread along the ground,
But not too hard or slacke, the meane is sweet,
Least slacke they snarle, or hard they proue
  vnsound,
And intermixt with siluer, silk or gold,‡
The tender hayres, the better so to hold.

---

* Arachne was so skilful a needlewoman that she challenged Minerva to a trial of skill, and hanged herself because the godless beat her. Minerva then changed her into a spider.

"Arachne's labours ne'er her hours divide,
Her noble hands nor looms nor spindles guide."
Hoole's "Jerusalem delivered," bk. ii.

† Knit the hair you mean to put in, one link at the rod's end, and divide them as equally as you can; put your three lowest fingers betwixt, and twine the knot; and your link shall be equally twist. If you wet your hair, it will twine better. A nimble hand, a weak and light rod that may be easily guided with one hand, needs but four or five hairs at the most for the greatest river fish, though a Salmon or a Luce,* so you have leng.h enough: and except the Luce and Salmon, these will suffice.—W. L.

‡ Intermixing with silver or gold is not good, because first, the thread and hair are not of equal reach. Secondly, the colours differing from the hairs or fly, affright the fish. Thirdly, they will not bend and twist with the hairs.—W. L.

---

* The full grown pike from the Latin Lucius, the wolf fish; hence Justice Shallow says:—The Luce is the fresh fish, the salt fish is an old coat ("Merry Wives of Windsor, I. i."), meaning Lucy is a new name, the old one was Charlecote.

Then end to end, as falleth to their lot
Let all your Linkes in order as they lie
Be knit together, with that Fishers knot
That will not slip or with the wet vntie:
And at the lowest end forget it not
To leaue a Bought or Compasse like an eye *
   The Linke that holds your Hooke to hang vpon,
   When you thinke good to take it off and on.

Which Linke must neither be so great nor strong,
Nor like of colour as the others were ; †
Scant halfe so big, so that it be as long:
Of grayest Hue, and of the soundest Hayre,
Least whiles it hangs the liquid waues among
The sight thereof, the warie Fish should feare.
   And at one end a Loope or Compasse fine,
   To fasten to the other of your line. ‡

---

* An upper end also, to put it to and fro the rod.—
W. L.

† The same colonr, to wit, grey like the sky ; the like bigness and strength, is good for all the line, and every link thereof! Weight is hurtful ; so unequal strength causeth the weakest to break.—W. L.

‡ For bottom fishing upright rings should be used. A fine gut foot line is better than a single horse hair, but the gut should be in its natural state, not drawn. Good gut is round, clear, hard, even, and almost colourless. Plain reels with a light check and 40 or 50 yards of fine dressed silk line complete the bottom fisher's equipment. In Nottingham fishing upright

Corke.

THEN take a good Corke, so much as shall suffice,
For euery Line to make his swimmer fit ;*
And where the midst and thickest parts doth rise,
There burne a round small hole quite thorow it :

---

rings, a wooden reel with seventy or eighty yards of Derby twist on it, and 4 or 5 feet of very fine gut are used. For spinning, stout upright rings and a plain winch with a moderate check, and 60 or 70 yards of medium sized dressed eight-plait line will be required. For trout fishing, a running line of hair and silk is preferable, and should be carefully tapered and be about 40 yards in length and in size be suited to the rod, neither too heavy nor too light. A plain check winch, not too wide between the plates, is far preferable to a multiplier. The casting line should vary with the weather : in shallow and clear water it should not be less than three yards. For salmon, tapered eight-plait dressed silk lines should be used and should never be less than 120 yards in length. The reel should be a common check winch, and the casting line should consist of three lengths of treble twisted gut, followed by two of good double gut, and then a single gut, in all about four yards in length.

* I utterly dislike your southern Corks. First, for they afright the fish in the bite and sight ; and because they follow not so kindly the nimble rod and hand. Secondly, they breed weight to the line ; which puts it in danger, hinders the nimble jerk of the rod, and loads the arm. A good eye and hand may easily discern the bite.—W. L.

And put therein a Quill of equall size,
But take good heed the Corke you doe not slit.
   Then round or square with Razor pare it neare,
   Piramid-wise, or like a slender Peare.

The smaller end doth serue to sinke more light,
Into the water with the Plummets sway;
The greater swimms aloft and stands vpright,
To keepe the Line and Bayt at euen stay,
That when the Fish begins to nib and byte,
The mouing of the float doth them bewray:*
   These may you place vpon your Lines at will,
   And stoppe them with a white and handsome Quill.

Hookes.

YOUR Hookes then buy the finest and the best
   That may be had of such as vse to sell,*
   And from the greatest to the very least

---

* For heavy streams use Cork floats of various weights, and for light streams use porcupine quills. A large float should be used for live baiting.

* I use to make mine own hooks; so that I shall have them of the best Spanish and Milan Needles of what size, bent and sharpness as I like and need. Soften your needles in a hot fire in a chafer. The instruments: First, an holdfast. Secondly, a

Of euery sort pike out and chuse them well,
Such as in shape and making passe the rest,
And doe for strength and soundnesse most excell:
  Then in a little Boxe of dryest wood
  From rust and canker keepe them faire and good.

That Hooke I loue that is in compasse round *
Like to the print that Pegasus did make,
With horned hoofe vpon Thessalian ground;
From whence forthwith Pernassus spring out brake,
That doth in pleasant Waters so abound:
  And of the Muses oft the thirst doth slake. †

---

hammer to flatten the place or the beard. Thirdly, a file to make the beard and sharpen the point. Fourthly, a bender, namely a pin bended, and put in the end of a stick an handful long.—When they are made, lap them in the end of a wire; heat them again, and temper them in oil or butter.—W. L.—(Dame Juliana Berners gives the process of hook-making in the greatest detail in her "Treatyse of Fysshynge.")

* The best form for ready striking and sure holding and strength, is a straight and somewhat long chank and straight nibbed; with a little compass: not round in any wise, for it neither strikes surely nor readily; but is weak, as having to great a compass. Some use to batter the upper end to hold the faster: But good thread or silk, well bound, may make it fast enough. It is botchery, hinders the biting, and sometimes cuts the line.—W. L.

† Pegasus was the winged horse on which Bellorophon rode against the Chimæra. When the Muses

Who on his fruitfull bankes doe sit and sing
That all the world of their swee[t] tunes doth
ring.

Or as Thaumantis, when she list to shroud
Her selfe against the parching sunny ray,
Vnder the mantle of some stormy cloud,
Where she her sundry colours doth display
Like Iunoes Bird, of her faire garments proud,
That Phœbus gaue her on her marriage day:
Shewes forth her goodly Circle farre and wide,
To mortall wights that wonder at her pride.

His shank should neither be to short nor long,
His point not ouersharpe, nor yet too dull:*
The substance good that may indure from wrong;
His Needle slender, yet both round and full,
Made of the right Iberian mettell strong,
That will not stretch nor breake at euery pull,
Wrought smooth and cleane withouten cracke
or knot†
And bearded like the wilde Arabian goat.

---

contended with the daughters of Pieros, Helicon rose
heavenward with delight ; but Pegasus gave it a kick,
stopped its ascent, and brought out of the mountain
the soul inspiring waters of Hippocrene.

* He means the hook may be too weak at the point.
It cannot be too sharp if the metal be good steel.—
W. L.

†Hooks are of various forms. There is the
Limerick bend, the Carlisle or round bend, the Sneck

Then let your Hooke be sure and strongly plaste
Vnto your lowest Linke with Silke or Hayre,
Which you may doe with often ouercaste,
So that you draw the Bouts together neare,
And with both ends make all the other fast,
That no bare place or rising knot appeare;
  Then on that Linke hang Leads of euen waight
  To raise your floate, and carry doune your baite.

Thus haue you Rod, Line, Float, and Hooke;
The Rod to strike, when you shall thinke it fit,
The Line to lead the Fish with wary skill,
The Float and Quill to warne you of the bit;
The Hooke to hold him by the chap or gill,
Hooke, Line, and Rod, all guided to your wit.
  Yet there remains of Fishing tooles to tell,
  Some other sorts that you must haue as well.

---

bend, and the Curved bend. I prefer the Limerick and Sneck, the former for Salmon and Trout fly fishing. When fishing for Trout with worm, I use the Sneck bend. For all other fishing, I prefer the Carlisle.

Other fishing Tooles.

A LITTLE Boord, the lightest you can finde,
But not so thin that it will breake or bend;
Of Cypres sweet, or of some other kinde,
That like a Trenchor shall it selfe extend:
Made smooth and plaine, your Lines thereon to winde*
With Battlements at euery other end:
Like to the Bulwarke of some ancient Towne,
As well-wald Sylchester now razed downe.†

A Shooe to beare the crawling Wormes therein,
With hole aboue to hang it by your side,‡

---

* Or wind them on two or three of your fingers like an Orph-Arion's string.—W. L.

† Silchester, in Berkshire, is Silicis Castrum (Flint-camp), a Saxon-Latin form of the Roman Calleva or Galleva. Galleva is the Roman form of the British *Gwal-Vawr* (great wall), so called from its wall, the ruins of which are still striking. According to tradition, King Arthur was crowned here; and Ninnius asserts that the City was built by Constantius, Father of Constantine the Great.

‡ Worm poke of cloth, or boxes.—W. L.

A hollow Cane that must be light and thin,
Wherein the Bobb and Palmer shall abide,
Which must be stopped with an handsome pin,
Least out againe your baytes doe hap to slide.
   A little Box that couered close shall lye,
   To keepe therein the busie winged Flye.

Then must you haue a Plummet, formed round,
Like to the Pellet of a birding Bow: *
Wherewith you may the secret'st waters sound,
And set your floate thereafter high, or low,
Till you the depth thereof haue truely found:
And on the same a twisted thread bestow
   At your owne will, to hang it on your hooke
   And so to let it downe into the Brooke.

Of Lead likewise, yet must you haue a Ring,
Whose whole Diameter in length containes
Three Inches full, and fastened to a string
That must be long and sure, if need constraines,†

---

* A plumet you need not; for your line being well leaded and without a float, will try your depths. When the lead above your hook comes to the earth, the line will leave sinking.—W. L.

‣ That is good: but a forked rod, about two yards long is better. When your hook is fastened in the water, take your forked rod, and put the line in the fork, and so follow down to your hook. So letting your line be somewhat slack, move your line to and fro, especially downwards; and so shall your fork be loosed.—W. L.

Through whose round hole you shall your Angle
  bring
And let it fall into the watry playne:
    Vntill he come the weedes and stickes vnto,
    From whence your hooke it serueth to vndo.*

Haue Tooles good store to serue your turne
  withall,
Least that you happen some to lose or breake;
As in great waters oft it doth befall,
When that the Hooke is nought or Line too
  weake.
And waxed thread, or silk, so it be small
To set them on, that if you list to wreake
    Your former losse, you may supply the place,
    And not returne with sorrow and disgrace.†

Haue twist likewise, so that it be not white,‡
Your Rod to mend, or broken top to tye;
For all white colours doe the Fishes fright
And make them from the bayte away to flye;

---

* The ring recommended in the poem is still the best method known of disengaging one's hook when caught.

† A most admirable piece of advice which should be taken to heart by all Anglers.

‡ White and grey are good, answering to the colours of the sky.—W. L.

A File to mend your hookes,‖ both small and light
A good sharpe knife, your girdle hanging by:
  A Pouch with many part and purses thin
  To carry all your Tooles and Trynkets in.

Yet must you haue a little Rip beside,
Of Willow twigs, the finest you can wish;
Which shall be made so handsome and so wide
As may containe good store of sundry Fish;
And yet with ease be hanged by your side
To bring them home the better to your dish.
  A little Net that on a Pole shall stand,
  The mighty Pike or heauy Carpe to Land.

His seuerall Tooles, and what garment is fittest.

AND let your garments Russet be or gray,
  Of colour darke, and hardest to discrye;
  That with the Raine or weather wil away,
And least offend the fearfull Fishes eye:

---

*A fine needle file is the kind to use, but they are to keen that a mere touch or two is all that is necessary.

For neither Skarlet nor rich cloth of ray,
Nor colours dipt in fresh Assyrian dye,
 Nor tender silkes of Purple, Paule, or golde,
 Will serue so well to keep off wet or colde.*

In this aray the Angler good shall goe.
Vnto the Brooke, to finde his wished game;
Like olde Menalcus wandering to and fro,
Vntill he chance to light vpon the same,

---

* " With regard to dress, some people are inclined to ridicule the idea of there being any necessity for attending to it at all. I am very sure, however, that excellent grounds exist for not being too conspicuous in this respect. The trout is a very gentlemanly fish, and does not like 'loud dressing ;' positive black and white, too, or anything which glitters or is unusual, should be carefully eschewed, particularly on the upper and more conspicuous part of the person. A tall black hat, or one of the genus called 'shiner,' I do not recommend ; and though I would rather fish in the Bishop of Winchester's stream than in his lordship's company when in full canonicals, I should equally consider Mr. Chadband in his cerements an objectionable party for successful trouting on a shy or wellfished stream ; while a stage coachman in a white top-coat and shiny hat would be fully as unacceptable. Brilliant paste buckles on the shoes I have no objecttion to if anyone likes them, but on the hat, no. I even dislike a highly-varnished rod. Who has not seen the flash of a rod waving in the air while half a mile distant ? and surely so unusual and startling a phenomenon cannot but be calculated to disturb the equanimity of so sharp-eyed a creature as the trout."— Francis, "On Angling," pp. 179-80.

And there his art and cunning shall bestow,
For euery Fish his Bayte so well to frame
   That long ere Phoebus set in Westerne fome
   He shall return well loaden to his home.

Obiection.

SOME youthfull Gallant here perhaps will say,
   This is no pastime for a gentleman.
It were more fit at cardes and dice to play,
To vse both fence and dauncing now and than,
Or walke the streetes in nice and strange Aray,
Or with coy phrases court his Mistris fan,
   A poore delight with toylle and painfull watch,
   With losse of time a silly Fish to catch.

What pleasure can it be to walk about,
The fields and meads and pinching cold?
And stand all day to catch a silly Trout,
That is not worth a teaster to be sold,
And peraduenture sometimes goe without,
Besides the toles and troubles manifold,
   And to be washt with many a showre of rayne
   Before he can returne from thence againe?

More ease it were, and more delight I trow,
In some sweet house to passe the time away

Amongst the best, with braue and gallant show,
And with faire dames to daunce, to sport and play,
And on the board the nimble dice to throw,
That brings in gaine, and helps the shot to pay,
 And with good wine and store of dainty fare,
 To feede at will and take but little care.

The Answere.

I MEANE not here mens errours to reproue,
 Nor doe enuie their seeming happy state;
 But rather meruaile why they doe not loue
 An honest sport that is without debate;
 Since their abused pastimes often moue
Their mindes to anger and to mortall hate:
 And as in bad delights their time they spend,
 So oft it brings them to no better end.

Indeed it is a life of lesser paine,
To sit at play from noone till it be night:
And then from night till it be noone againe.
With damned oathes, pronounced in despight,
For little cause and euery trifle vaine,
To curse, to brawle, to quarrell, and to fight,
 To packe the cardes, and with some cozning trick
 His fellowes Purse of all his coyne to picke.

Or to beguile another of his Wife,
As did Æghistus Agamemnon scrue:
Or as that Roman Monarch* led a life
To spoyle and spend, while others pine and sterue,
And to compell their friends with foolish strife
To take more drinke then will their health preserue,
 And to conclude, for debt or iust desart,
 In baser tune to sing the counter-part.

O let me rather on the pleasant Brinke
Of Tyne and Trent possesse some dwelling place;
Where I may see my Quill and Corke downe sinke,
With eager bit of Barbill, Bleike, or Dace:
And on the World and his Creator thinke,
While they proud Thais painted sheat imbrace.
 And with the fume of strong Tobacco's smoke,
 And quaffing round are ready for to choke.

Let them that list these pastimes then pursue,
And on their pleasing fancies feed their fill;
So I the Fields and Meadowes greene may view,
And by the Riuers freshe may walke at will,
Among the Dayzes and the Violets blew:
Red Hyacinth, and yealow Daffadill,
 Purple Narcissus, like the morning rayes,
 Pale Ganderglas, and azour Culuerkayes.

---
* Nero.

I count it better pleasure to behold
The goodly compasse of the loftie skye,
And in the midst thereof like burning gold
The flaming chariot of the worlds great eye;
The watry cloudes that in the ayre vprold
With sundry kindes of painted collours flie:
    And fayre Aurora lifting vp her head,
    And blushing rise from old Thitonus bed.

The hills and Mountains raised from the Plaines,
The plaines extended leuell with the ground,
The ground deuided into sundry vaines,
The vaines inclos'd with running riuers round,
With headlong course into the sea profounde:
    The surging sea beneath the valleys low,
    The valleys sweet, and lakes that louely flowe.

The lofty woods the forrests wide and long,
Adornd with leaues and branches fresh and greene
In whose coole bow'rs the birds with chaunting song,
Doe welcome with their quire the Summers Queene,
The meadowes faire where Flora's gifts among,
Are intermixt the verdant grasse betweene,
    The siluer skaled fish that softlie swimme,
    Within the brookes and christall watry brimme.

All these and many more of his creation,
That made the heauens the Anglers oft doth see,

And takes therein no little delectation,
To thinke how strange and wonderfull they be,
Framing thereof an inward contemplation,
To set his thoughts from other fancies free,
  And whiles he lookes on these with ioyfull eye,
  His minde is wrapt aboue the starry skye.

The Author of Angling.

BVT how this Art of Angling did beginne,
    And who the vse thereof and practise found,
    How many times and ages since have bin,
Wherein the sunne hath dayly compast round
The circle that the signes twice sixe are in:
And yeelded yearely comfort to the ground,
  It were too hard for me to bring about,
  Since Ouid wrote not all story out.

Yet to content the willing Readers eare,
I will not spare the sad report to tell,
When good Deucalion and his Pirrha deere,
Were onely left vpon the earth to dwell
Of all the rest that ouerwhelmed were
With that great floud, that in their dayes befell,
  Wherein the compasse of the world so round
  Both man and beast with waters deepe were dround.

Between themselues they wept and made great
  moane,
How to repaire againe the wofull fall,
Of all mankinde, whereof they two alone
The remnant were, and wretched portion small.
But any meanes or hope in them was none,
That might restore so great a losse with all,
  Since they were aged, and in yeares so runne,
  That now almost their threed of life was spunne.

Vntill at last they saw where as they stood
An ancient Temple wasted and forlorne;
Whose holy fires and sundry offerings good,
The late outragious waues away had borne;
But when at length doune fallen was the flood,
The waters low it proudly gan to scorne.
  Vnto that place they thought it best to goe
  The counsell of the Goddesse there to know.

For long before that fearfull Deluge great,
The vniuersall Earth had ouerfloune;
A heauenly power there placed had her seate,
And ansueres gaue of hidden things vnknowne.
Thither they went her fauour to intreat,
Whose fame throughout that coast abroad was
  bloune
  By her aduice some way or meane to finde,
  How to renew the race of human kinde.

Prostrate they fell vpon the sacred ground,
Kissing the stones, and shedding many a teare;
And lowly bent their aged bodies doune
Vnto the earth, with sad and heauy cheare:
Praying the Saint with soft and dolefull sound
That she vouchsafe their humble suite to heare
   The goddesse heard, and bad them goe and take,
   Their mothers bones, and throw behind their backe.

This Oracle obscure, and dark of sence,
Amazed much their mindes with feare and doubt,
What kind meaning might be drawne from thence;
And how to vnderstande and finde it out,
How with so great a sinne they might dispence
Their Parents bones to cast and throw about:
   Thus when they had long time in study spent,
   Out of the Church with carefull thought they went.

And now beholding better euery place,
Each Hill and Dale, each Riuer, Rock, and Tree;
And muzing thereupon a little space,
They thought the Earth their mother well might be,
And that the stones that lay before their face,
To be her bones did nothing disagree:

Wherefore to proue if it were false or true,
The scattered stones behind their backes they
    threw.

Forthwith the stones (a wondrous thing to heare,)
Began to moue as they had life conceiu'd.
And waxed greater then at first they were;
And more and more the shape of man receiu'd
Till euery part most plainly did appeare,
That neither eye nor sence could be deceiu'd:
    They heard, they spake, they went and walked
        too,
    As other liuing men are wont to doe.

Thus was the earth replenished a new,
With people strange, sprung vp with little paine,
Of whose increase the progenie that grew,
Did soone supply the empty world againe;
But now a great care there did insue,
How such a mightie number to maintaine,
    Since foode there was not any to be found,
    For that great flood had all destroyed and
        drownd.

Then did Deucalion first the Art inuent
Of Angling, and his people taught the same;
And to the Woods and groues with them hee went
Fit tooles to finde for this most needfull game;

There from the trees the longest ryndes they rent,
Wherewith strong Lines they roughly twist and
frame,
 And of each crooke of hardest Bush and Brake,
 They made them Hookes the hungry Fish to
take.

And to intice them to the eager bit,
Dead frogs and flies of sundry sorts he tooke;
And snayles and wormes such as he found most
fit
Wherein to hide the close and deadly hooke:
And thus with practice and inuentive wit,
He found the meanes in euery lake and brooke
 Such store of Fish to take with little paine,
 As did long time this people new sustaine.

In this rude sort began this simple Art,
And so remain'd in that first age of old,
When Saturne did Amaltheas horne impart
Vnto the world, that then was all of Gold;
The Fish as yet had felt but little smart,
And were to bite more eager, apt and bold:
 And plentie still supplide the place againe
 Of woefull want, whereof we now complaine.

But when in time the feare and dread of man
Fell more and more on euery liuing thing,

And all the creatures of the world began
To stand in awe of this vsurping King,
Whose tyranny so farre extended than
That Earth and Seas it did in thraldome bring;
   It was a worke of greater paine and skill,
   The wary Fish in lake or Brooke to kill.

So worse and worse two ages more did passe,
Yet still the Art more perfect daily grew,
For then the slender Rod inuented was,
Of finer sort than former ages knew,
And Hookes were made of siluer and of brasse,
And Lines of Hempe and Flaxe were framed new,
   And sundry baites experience found out more,
   Then elder times did know or try before.

But at the last the Iron age drew neere,
Of all the rest the hardest, and most scant,
Then Lines were made of Silke and subtile hayre,
And Rods of lightest Cane and Hazell plant,
And Hookes of hardest steel inuented were,
That neither skill nor workmanship did want,
   And so this Art did in the end attaine
   Vnto that state where now it doth remaine.

But here my weary Muse a while must rest.
That is not vsed to so long a way;

And breath, or pause a little at the least
At this Lands end, vntill another day,
And then againe, if so she thinke it best;
Our taken-taske afresh, wee will assay,
   And forward goe as wee did intend
   Till that wee come vnto our iourneys end.

THE END OF THE FIRST BOOKE.

Bibliotheca Curiosa.

THE
Secrets of Angling;

TEACHING
THE CHOICEST TOOLS, BAITS,
AND SEASONS,
FOR THE TAKING OF ANY FISH
IN
POND OR RIVER,

Practised and familiarly opened
in three Books,

BY
J. D., Esquire,

EDITED BY "PISCATOR."

VOL. II.

PRIVATELY PRINTED, EDINBURGH.

1885.

Secrets of Angling.

Bibliotheca Curiosa.

THE
Secrets of Angling;

TEACHING

THE CHOICEST TOOLS, BAITS,
AND SEASONS,
FOR THE TAKING OF ANY FISH
IN
POND OR RIVER,

Practised and familiarly opened
in three Books,

BY

J. D., Esquire.

EDITED BY "PISCATOR."

Vol. II.

PRIVATELY PRINTED, EDINBURGH
1885.

THE
Secrets of Angling.

The second Booke.

BEFORE, I taught what kind of Tooles were fit
   For him to have that would an Angler be;
   And how he should with practise and with wit
Prouide himself thereof in best degree:
Now doth remaine to shew how to the bit
The Fishes may be brought, that earst were free.
   And with what pleasing baits intis'd they are,
   To swallow downe the hidden Hooke vnware.

Baites.

IT were not meet to send a Huntsman out
    Into the Woods, with Net, with Gin, or
        Hay,
    To trace the brakes and bushes all about,
    The Stag, the Foxe, or Badger, to betray:
If hauing found his game, he stand in doubt
Which way to pitch, or where his snares to lay,
    And with what traine he may entise withall
    The fearefull beast into his trap to fall.

So, though the Angler haue good store of tooles,
And them with skill in finest sort can frame ;
Yet when he comes to Riuers, Lakes, and Pooles,
If that he know not how to vse the same,
And with what baites to make the Fishes fooles,
He may goe home as wise as out he came,
    And of his comming boast himselfe as well
    As he that from his fathers Chariot fell.

Not that I take vpon me to impart
More than by others hath before beene told :
Or that the hidden secrets of this Art
I would unto the vulgar sort vnfolde,
Who peraduenture for my paines desart
Would count me worthy Balams horse to holde :
    But onely to the willing learner show
    So much thereof us may suffise to know.

But here, O Neptune, that with triple Mace
Dost rule the raging of the Ocean wide;
I meddle not with thy deformed race
Of monsters huge, that in those waues abide:
With that great Whale, that by three whole dayes
  space
The man of God did in his belly hide,
  And cast him out vpon the Euxin shore,
  As safe and sound as he had beene before.

Nor with that Orke that on Cephæan strand
Would haue deuour'd Andromeda the faire,
Whom Perseus slew with strong and valiant
  hand,
Deliuering her from danger and despaire,
The Hurlepool huge that higher then the land,
Whole streames of water spouteth in the ayre,
  The Porpois large that playing swims on hie,
  Portending stormes or other tempests nie.

Nor that admirer of sweet Musicke's sound,
That on his backe Arion bore away;
And brought to shore out of the Seas profound,
The Hippotame that like an horse doth neigh,
The Mors, that from the rockes inrolled round,
Within his teeth himselfe doth safe conuay:
  The Tortoise couered with his target hard,
  The Tuberone attended with his guard.

Nor with that Fish that beareth in his snout
A ragged sword, his foes to spoile and kill;
Nor that fierce Thrasher, that doth fling about
His nimble flayle, and handles him at will:
The rauenous Sharke that with the sweepings out
And filth of ships doth oft his belly fill.
   The Albacore that followeth night and day
   The flying Fish, and takes them for his prey.

The Crocodile that weepes when he doth wrong,
The Hollibut that hurts the appetite,
The Turbut broad, the Sceale, the Sturgion strong,
The Cod and Cozze, that greedy are to bite,
The Haake the Haddocke, and Conger long,
The yeallow Ling, the Milwell faire and white,
   The spreading Ray, the Thornback thin and flat,
   The boysterous Base, the hoggish Tunny fat.

These kindes of Fish that are so large of sise,
And many more that here I leave vntolde
Shall goe for me, and all the rest likewise
That are the stocke of Proteus watry folde :
For well I thinke my Hookes would not suffise,
Nor slender Lines, the least of these to holde.
   I leaue them therefore to the surging seas,
   In that huge depth to wander at their ease.

And speak of such as in the fresh are found,
The little Roach, the Menise biting fast,
The slymie Tench, the slender Smelt and round,
The Vmber sweet, the graueling good of taste,
The wholesome Ruffe, the Barbill not so sound,
The Pearch and Pike that all the rest doe waste,
  The Bream, the Carpe, the Chub, and Chau-
    ender,
  And many more that in fresh waters are.

Sit then Thalia on some pleasant banke,
Among so many as faire Auon hath,
And marke the Anglers how they march in ranke,
Some out of Bristoll, some from healthfull Bath,
How all the Riuers sides along they flanke,
And through the meadowes make their wonted
    path :
  See how their wit and cunning they apply,
  To catch the Fish that in the waters lye.

For the Goodgion.

LOE, in a little Boate where one doth
    stand,
  That to a Willow Bough the while is
    tide,
  And with a pole doth stirre and raise
the sand ;
Whereas the gentle streame doth softly slide,

And then with slender Line and Rod in hand,
The eager bit not long he doth abide.
  Well leaded is his Line, his Hooke but small,
  A good big Corke to beare the streame withall.

His baite the least red worme that may be found
And at the bottome it doth alwayes lye ;
Whereat the greedy Goodgion bites so sound
That Hooke and all he swalloweth by and by : *
See how he strikes, and puls them vp as round
As if new store the play did still supply.
  And when the bit doth dye or bad doth proue.
  Then to another place he doth remoue.

This Fish the fittest for a learner is
That in this Art delights to take some paine ;
For as high flying Haukes that often misse
The swifter soules, are eased with a traine,
So to a young beginner yeeldeth this,
Such readie sport as makes him proue againe,
  And leades him on with hope and glad desire.
  To greater skill and cunning to aspire.†

---

* The Gudgeon hath his teeth in his throat (as also the Chub), and lives by much sucking. He is a dainty fish, like, or nearly as good as the Sparling.—W. L.

† Gudgeon bite best in clear water and warm weather in moderately rapid streams, where the water ranges from two to four or five feet in depth.

For the Roche.

THEN see on yonder side, where one doth sit
With Line well twisted, and his Hooke but small;
His Corke not big, his Plummets round and fit,
His bayte of finest paste, a little ball
Wherewith he doth intice vnto the bit,
The carelesse Roche* that soone is caught with all:
Within a foote the same doth reach the ground,
And with least touch the float straight sinketh downe.

In order to attract them it is necessary to rake up the gravel so as to cause a thick water. The gudgeon immediately flock to the spot to feed upon the small insects and worms that are thus exposed. For this purpose a heavy iron rake with a long handle is used. The angler then fishes over the raked spot, his bait just tripping over the bottom. A light cork float and a No. 10 hook are advisable. The gudgeon feeds upon gentles, or any small grubs, and worms; but nothing can compare in point of attraction to a small fragment of red worm. The gudgeon is a most agreeable acquaintance at the breakfast table. There is a crispness and piquancy about his discussion, when duly fried and neatly served, which is highly gratifying.

* The Roach is one of the meanest (fish).—W. L.

And as a skilful Fowler that doth vse,
The flying Birds of any kinde to take,
The fittest and the best doth alwayes chuse,
Of many sorts a pleasing stale to make,
Which if he doth perceiue they doe refuse,
And of mislike abandon and forsake,
  To win their loue againe, and get their grace
  Forthwith doth put another in the place.

So for the Roach more baites he hath beside,
As of a sheepe the thicke congealed blood,
Which on a board he vseth to deuide
In portions small to make them fit and good,
That better on his hooke they may abide :
And of the waspe the white and tender brood.
  And wormes that breed on euery hearbe and
    tree,
  And sundry flies that quicke and liuely be.*

---

* Roach-fishing is very pretty sport, requiring the exercise of much skill, patience, quickness of apprehension, and ingenuity, combined with a thorough knowledge of the habits of the fish. No greater mistake can be made than to fancy the roach is a simple fish. When he is half-starved, and seldom fished for, he is no doubt easy to capture. When about to spawn or just spent, he loses much of his caution and shyness ; but when he is well fed, in high condition, and sees many rods, he becomes amazingly shy of the hook. I am the tenant of a portion of a river in which thousands of splendid roach may be seen in great shoals. It was a long time before I could

For the Dace.

THEN looke where as that Poplar gray doth grow,
Hard by the same where one doth closely stand,
And with the winde his Hooke and bayt doth throw
Amid the streame with slender hazell wand,

---

get on terms with these roach. In summer and in clear water it was hopeless. If you could get a tree at your back, you might catch two or three, but that would be a signal for the rest to disperse. In coloured water, however, and more particularly in winter, I found at last that after three or four days' baiting, and with single hair, I could give a good account of them, and I made some splendid takes, though they are still very capricious. The hook, if the water be full and the fish biting freely, should be a No. 9, to carry two gentles. If the water be very clear, and the fish shy, a No. 10 or 11 hook, to take only one gentle, will be found preferable. The best hook-baits for roach are, first, maggots, or gentles, as they are more commonly called by metropolitan anglers. Those blown on bullock's liver, which are shiny and yellow, are the best by far. When using them, the roach, not being hungry, often want a little coaxing or variety. When you think this is the case, instead of two gentles use one, and point your hook with a chrysalis. The next most favourite pabulum with roach are pearl-barley and then paste.

Where as he sees the Dace themselues doe show,
His eye is quicke, and ready is his hand,
   And when the Fish doth rise to catch the bayt,
   He presently doth strike, and takes her strayt.

O worlds deceit! how are we thrald by thee.
That dost thy gall in sweetest pleasures hide?
When most we thinke in happiest state to be,
Then doe we soonest into danger slide,
Behold the Fish that euen now was free,
Vnto the deadly hooke how he is tide,
   So vaine delights alure vs to the snare,
   Wherein vnwares we fast intangled are.*

Some prefer paste; I prefer pearl-barley. The red worm is a tolerably good bait also for roach, particularly in thick water, where the fish may have been feeding on worms, and the large roach will often in winter take the tail of a lob worm very ravenously. Caddis bait is also a favourite bait with roach, but it is a bad substitute for gentles. The diminutive bloodworm, found in the muddy deposit at the bottom of stagnant waters, is held to be a great attraction for roach, but it requires a fine hook and great care to bait it well.—Francis *On Angling*, pp. 23-9.

* By August, on the Thames, they get on the shallows, where they may be taken in large numbers, by whipping with almost any small fly, or even with a single gentle; some people, to make the fly more attractive, point the hook with a gentle; others, as I have recommended in roach-fishing, use a small shred of kid or wash-leather. I have found the inner rind of a scrap of stringy bacon answer better perhaps than

For the Carpe.

BVT now againe see where another stands,
 And straines his rod that double seemes
  to bend,
 Loe how he leades and guides him
  with his hands,
Least that his Line should breake or Angle rend,
Then with a Net see how at last he lands,
A mighty Carpe * and has him in the end,
 So large he is of body, scale, and bone,
 That rod and all had like to haue beene gone.

---

either, being a kind of compromise between the two; that is, something to taste, and not liable to be whipped off. A short stiff rod (about eight feet long) is the best for this work. The line should not be too long, or it is not manageable, as quick striking is the order of the day with this very nimble fish. The flies should always be dressed upon as large hooks as the angler can afford to dress them on, as the fish rising often in very sharp streams are apt to break off from any slight hold. They are fairly delicate fish to eat when in good order, and should be broiled dry, a slice of butter being then allowed to melt upon them. They make one of the most valuable spinning baits for jack and trout which the angler can obtain, being bright and round, and reasonably tough on the hooks. —Francis *On Angling*, pp. 35-37.

* It is not natural to see the bait hanging in the water barely touching the bottom, and that the carp know well enough. In this position the gut ascends directly from the worm to the float, and the unnatural

Marke what a line he hath, well made and strong,
Of Bucephall, or Bayards, strongest hayre,
Twisted with greene or watched silke among,
Like hardest twine, that holds the intangled Deare,
Not any force of Fish will doe it wrong,
In Tyne, or Trent, or Thame, he needes not feare :
  The knots of euery lincke are knit so sure,
  That many a plucke and pull they may indure.

His corke is large, made handsome, smooth, and fine,
The leads according, close, and fit thereto,
A good round hooke set on with silken twine,
That will not slip nor easily vndoe :

---

attitude of the bait challenges the carp's attention to this 'new thing in baits.' Mons. Carp then catches sight of the shot, and, lastly, in all probability, of the float above. All this is of course strange and unusual, and he proceeds to investigate the bait with all due care, nibbling and picking at it, like the female ghoul in the Arabian Nights, who ate rice with a bodkin ; he cannot make up his mind to take it, and yet he cannot make up his mind to leave it, so he nibbles and nibbles, and at last you think he must have got the bait, and you strike. Now, it is not customary for baits to dash off in that frantic fashion ; and therefore, while your bait dashes off one way, Master Carp dashes off the other.—Francis *On Angling*, pp. 77-8.

His bait great wormes that long in mosse haue bin,
Which by his side he beareth in a shooe.
  Or paste wherewith he feedes him oft before,
  That at the bottom lyes a foote or more.*

for the Chub and Trout.

SEE where another hides himselfe as slye,
  As did Acteon, or the fearefull Deere;
  Behinde a withy, and with watchfull eye
  Attends the bit within the water cleere,
  And on the top thereof doth moue his flye,
With skilfull hand, as if he liuing were †
  Loe how the Chub, the Roche the Dace and Trout,
  To catch thereat doe gaze and swimme about.

His Rod, or Cane, made darke for being seene,
The lesse to feare the warie Fish withall:
His Line well twisted is, and wrought so cleane,
That being strong, yet doth it shew but small,

---

* The baits for Carp are the same as for Gudgeon. Paste can also be used. Potatoe is not to be despised, but after all Carp are of no value except for sport, tasting remarkably like a sheep's fleece in a very dirty state. This with every apology to Dame Berners, who calls him a "deyntous fish."

† Diversely. For the trout is a ravening fish, and and at that time of the day comes from his hole, if he come at all.—W. L.

His Hooke not great, nor little, but betweene,*
That light vpon the watry brimme may fall,

---

* The Trout makes the Angler the most gentlemanly and readiest sport of all other fishes : if you angle with a made fly, and a line twice your rod's length or more, of three hairs, in a plain water without wood, in a dark windy day from mid-afternoon, and have learned the cast of the fly.

Your fly must counterfeit the May Fly, which is bred of the cad bait ; and is called the Water Fly. You must change his colour every month ; beginning with a dark white and so grow to a yellow. The form cannot so well be put on a paper, as it may be taught by sight.

The head is of black silk or hair; the wings of a feather of a mallard, teal, or pickled hen's wing ; the body of crewel according to the month for colour, and run about with a black hair : all fastened at the tail with a thread that fastened the hook. You must fish in or by the stream, and have a quick hand, a ready eye and a nimble rod. Strike with him! or you lose him.

If the wind be rough, and trouble the crust of the water : he will take it in the plain deeps : and then and there commonly the greatest may rise. When you have hooked him, give him leave ! keeping your line straight. Hold him from the roots, and he will tire himself. This is the chief pleasure of Angling.

This fly, and two links, among wood, or close by a bush, moved in the crust of the water, is deadly in an evening, if you come close [*hidden*]. This is called " Busking for Trout."

Cad bait is a worm bred under stones in a shallow river : or in some out-runner of the river, where the

The Line in length scant halfe the Rod exceedes,
And neither Corke, nor Leade thereon it needes.*

---

streams run not strongly in a black shale. They stick by heaps on the side of a great stone, it being hollow. They be ripe in the beginning of May : they are pats with July. They be yellow when they be ripe, and have a black head. This is a deadly bait for a Trout either aloft [*on the surface*] or at the ground ; if your tools be fine and you come close : for the Trout of all other fish, is most affrighted with sight. And indeed it should be considered that fish are afraid of any extraordinary motion or sight of whatsoever colour : except the Pike ; which will be open to your sight on a sunshiny day, till you halter him.

The Trout will take also the worm, menise or any bait : so will the Pike, save that he will not take the fly.—W .L.

* To attempt to give any information about trout-fishing within the compass of a note would be like the task set by a celebrated headmaster to his form, "To write an essay on Universal History." Mr. Francis, in his book "On Angling," Messrs. Stewart, Pennell, Younger, Stodart, and others have written volumes on the subject, but I would strongly recommend a book which has lately appeared by one of the finest fishermen to be met with on Clyde or Tweed, the "Angler and the loop rod" by D. Webster, Edinburgh, 1885. Every possible information, and that of the most reliable character will be found in its pages.

For the Troute, and Eele.

NOW see some standing where the streame doth fall,
With headlong course behind the sturdy weere,
That ouerthwart the riuer, like a wall,
The water stops and strongly vp doth beare,
And at the Tayles, of Mills and Arches small.
Whereas the shoote is swift and not too cleare,
 Their lines in length not twice aboue an ell,
But with good store of lead and twisted well.

Round handsome hookes that will not breake nor bend
The big red worme, well scowred, is their bayte,
Which doune vnto the bottome doth discend,
Whereas the Trout and Eele * doth lye in wayte,

---

* There be divers ways to catch the wrinkling Eel. Your Line must be stronger—six or seven hairs—and your hook accordingly: for she must upon the hooking presently [*immediately*] be drawn forth with force: otherwise she fastens herself with her tail about a root or stone or such like; and so you lose your labour, your hook, and the fish. The worm or menise are her common bait.

There is a way to catch Eels by "Braggling:" thus. Take a rod, small and tough of sallow, hazel or such like, a yard long, as big as a beanstalk. In

And to their feeding busily intend,
Which when they see they snatch and swallow
    straight.

---

the small end thereof, make a nick or cleft with a knife ; in which nick put your strong but little hook baited with a red worm ; and made sure to a line of ten or twelve good hairs, but easily that the Eels may pull it out.

Go into some shallow place of the river among the great stones, and braggle up and down till you find holes under the stones. There put in your hook so baited at your rod's end, and the Eel under the stone will not fail to take it. Give her time to put it over ; and then, if your strength will serve, she is your own.

There is a third usual way to catch Eels, called "Bobbing." Upon a long and double strong thread, two yards long or thereabouts, spit some many great red worms—gotten in a summer's evening with a candle—as the thread will hold lengthways through the midst, and link them about your hand like a rope, and fasten these to a long goad's end with a cord as long as your rod ; and a great plummet of lead, a handful above the "Bob."

In a troubled or flooded river, in a deep tun, or by a stream side ; let it fall within a handbreadth of the ground : and then shall you sensibly feel a multitude of Eels, all in that pit, like so many dogs at a carrion ; tug and pull. Now at your good time, when you think that every Eel hath got a link and swallowed it up—like so many ducks the entrails of a pullet—draw up very easily, and they will follow working and pulling ; till you have them near the crust : and then amain hoist them to land. This is the readiest way where Eels are plentiful, to catch many.

Vpon their lines is neither Corke nor Quill,
But when they feele them plucke then strike
    they stil.*

For the Sewant and Flounder.

BEHOLD some others ranged all along,
    To take the Sewant yea, the Flounder
        sweet,
    That to the banke in deepest places
        throng,

For the Trout, you shall find in the root of a great
dock a white worm with a red head. With this,
fish for a Trout at the ground.—W. L.

* Stichering is yet another method of catching
eels. It is, I think, peculiar to Hampshire, as I never
heard of it elsewhere; but there is a good deal of fun
at times in a stichering party. The apparatus used is
an old sickle, worn short and chipped so as to be
roughly toothed. This is tied on to a light pole some
twelve feet long. Armed with one of these and a
bag the sportsman sallies forth to the water meadows,
where the wide deep drains for irrigating purposes are
situated. Peering about, at the bottom of one of
these, he presently espies an eel, or the head of one,
projecting from under a leaf or weed; he then gently
and cautiously thrusts the hook under the eel's body,
and with a sudden toss pitches him high and dry on
the bank, and puts him in the bag. An unskilful
sticherer will sometimes chop off his neighbour's ear,
or poke out his eye, which doubtless lends excitement
to the sport.—Francis *On Angling*, p. 90.

To shunne the swifter streame that runnes so
   fleete,
And lye and feede the brackish waues among,
Whereas the waters fresh and salt doe meete :
   And there the Eele and Shad sometimes is
      caught
   That with the tide into the brookes are brought.

But by the way it shall not be amisce,
To vnderstand that in the waters gray,
Of floating Fish, two sundry kindes there is;
The one that liues by rauen and by pray,
And of the weaker sort, now that, now this,
He bites, and spoyles, and kills, and beares away,
   And in his greedy gullet doth deuoure,
   As Scillas gulfe, a ship within his powre.

And these haue wider mouths to catch and take
Their flying pray, whom swiftly they pursew,
And rowes of teeth like to a saw or rake,
Wherewith their gotten game they bite and chew,
And greater speede within the waters make,
To set vpon the other simple crew,
   And as the grayhound steales vpon the hare,
   So doe they vse to rush on them vnware.

Vnequall Fate, that some are borne to be
Fearefull and milde, and for the rest a pray,
And others are ordain'd to liue more free,
Without controule or danger any way :

So doth the Foxe the Lambe destroy we see,
The Lyon fierce, the Beauer, Roe, or Gray,
   The Hauke, the foule, the greater wrong the lesse
   The lofty proud, the lowly poore oppresse.

For the Pike or Pearch.

NOW for to take this kinde of Fish with all,[*]
   It shalbe needfull to haue still in store,
   Some liuing baites as Bleikes and Roches small,
Goodgion or Loach, not taken long before,
Or yealow Frogges that in the waters craule,
But all aliue they must be evermore:
   For as for baites that dead and dull doe lye,
   They least esteeme and set but little by.

But take good heed your line be sure and strong,
The knots well knit, and of the soundest hayre,
Twisted with some well coloured silk among,
And that you haue no neede your Rod to feare ;
For these great Fish will striue and struggle long,
Rod, line, and all into the streame to beare.

---

[*] A young whelp, kitling, or such like, is good bait for the Luce.—W. L.

And that your hooke be not too small and
    weake,
Least that it chance to stretch, or hap to
    breake.

And as in Arden or the mountains hoare,
Of Appennine or craggy Alps among,
The mastifes fierce that hunt the bristled Boare,
Are harnesed with Curats light and strong,
So for these Fish your line a foote or more,
Must armed be with thinnest plate along,
    Or slender wyre well fastned thereunto,
    That will not slip or easily vndoe.

The other kinde that are vnlike to these
Doe liue by corne, or any other seede :
Some times by crummes of bread, of paste or
    cheese,
Or grassehoppers that in greene meadowes breed,
With brood of waspes, of hornets, doares or bees,
Lip berries from the bryar bush or weede,
    Bloud wormes, and snayles, or crauling lentiles
        small,
    And buzzing flies that on the waters fall.

All these are good and many others more,
To make fit baites to take these kinde of Fish,
So that some faire deepe place you feede before,
A day or two, with paile, with bole, or dish ;

And of these meats doe vse to throw in store,
Then shall you haue them byte as you would
  wish.
  And ready sport to take your pleasure still,
  Of any sort that best you like to kill.

Thus seruing them as often as you may,
But once a weeke at least it must be done,
If that to bite they make too long delay,
As by your sport may be perceived soone :
Then some great Fish doth feare the rest away,
Whose fellowship and companie they shunne :
  Who neither in the bait doth take delight,
  Nor yet will suffer them that would to byte.

For this you must a remedie prouide,
Some Roche, or Bleike, as I haue shew'd before
Beneath whose vpper fin you close shall hide
Of all your Hooke the better halfe and more,
And though the point appeare or may be spide,
It makes no matter any whit therefore :
  But let him fall into the watry brimme,
  And downe vnto the bottome softly swimme.

And when you see your Corke begin to moue,
And round about to soare and fetch a ring,
Sometime to sinke, and sometime swimme aboue,
As doth the Ducke within the watry spring.

Yet make no haste your present hap to proue,
Till with your float at last away hee fling,
  Then may you safely strike and hold him
    short,
  And at your will prolong or end your sport.

But euery Fish loues not each bayte alike,
Although sometime they feede vpon the same ;
But some doe one, and some another seeke,
As best vnto their appetite doth frame,
The Roche, the Bream, the Carpe, the Chub and
  Bleik,
With paste or corne, their greedy hunger tame,
  The Dace, the Ruffe, the Goodgion and the
    rest,
  The smaller sort of crawling wormes loue
    best.

The Chauender and Chub doe more delight*
To feede on tender Cheese or Cherries red,
Blacke snayles, their bellies slit to shew their
  white,
Or grashoppers that skip in euery Meade,
The Pearch, the Tench, and Eele, doe rather
  bite
At great red wormes, in Field or Garden bred,

---

  * The Chavender is another name for Chub.

That have beene scowr'd in mosse or Fenell
    rough,
To rid their filth, and make them hard and
    tough.

And with this bayte hath often taken bin
The Salmon faire of Riuer-fish the best;
The Shad, that in the spring time cometh in,
The Suant swift, that is not set by least,
The Bocher sweet the pleasant Flounder thin
The Peele, the Tweat, the Botling, and the
    rest,
  With many more that in the deepe doth lye.
  Of Auon, Vske, of Seuerne, and of Wye.

Alike they bite, alike they pull downe low
The sinking Corke that striues to rise againe,
And when they feele the sudden deadly blow,
Alike they shunne the danger and the paine.
And as an arrow from the Scithian bow,
All flee alike into the streame amaine,
  Vntill the Angler by his wary skill
    There tyres them out, and brings them vp at
    will.

Yet further more it doth behove to know,
That for the most part Fish doe seeke their
    foode

Vpon the ground, or deepest bottome low,
Or at the top of water, streame, or flood;
And so you must your hooke and bayte bestow,
For in the midst you shall doe little good,
  For heaue things downe to the bottom fall,
  And light doe swim, and seldome sinke at all.

All summer long aloft the Fishes swimme,
Delighted with faire Phœbus shining ray,
And lye in wayte within the waters dimme
For flyes and gnats that on the top doe play,
Then halfe a yard beneath the vpper brimme
It shall be best your bayted Hooke to lay,
  With gnat or flye of any sort or kinde,
  That euery Moneth on Leaues or Trees you finde.

But then your Line must haue no Lead at all,
And but a slender Corke, or little Quill,
To stay the bayte that downe it doe not fall,
But hang a Linke within the water still,
Or else vpon the top thereof you shall
With quicker hand, and with more ready skill
  Let fall your flye, and now and then remoue,
  Which soone the Fish will finde and better loue.

And in the streame likewise they vse to be
At tailes of floudgates, or at Arches wide:

Or shallow flats, whereas the waters free
With fresher springs and swifter course doe
    slide:
And then of Waspe, the brood that cannot flye
Vpon a Tyle stone first a little dryed,
  Or yealow bobs turned vp before the Plough
  Are chiefest bayts, with Corke and Lead
    enough.

But when the golden Chariot of the Sunne,
Departing from our Northern countries fare
Beyond the ballance, now his course hath runne,
And goes to warme the cold Antarticq starre,
And Summer's heat is almost spent and done
With new approach of Winters dreadfull warre:
  Then doe the Fish withdraw into the deepe.
  And low from sight and cold more close doe keepe.

Then on your Lines you may haue store of Lead,
And bigger Corkes of any size you will,
And where the Fish are vsed to be fed
There shall you lay vpon the bottom still.
And whether that your bayte be corne, or bread,
Or Wormes, or Paste, it doth not greatly skill.
  For these alone are to be vsed then,
    Vntill the spring or summer come againe.

Thus haue I shew'd how Fish of diuers kinde
Best taken are, and how their bayts to know:

But Phœbus now beyond the Westerne Inde,
Beginneth to descend and draweth low,
And well the weather serues and gentle winde
Doune with the tide and pleasant streame to row,
  Vnto some place where we may rest vs in,
  Vntill we shall another time begin.*

---

* Our Author really gives very little information as to Pike and Perch fishing, so I have added, as an Appendix, some few particulars, mostly drawn from " A book on Angling" by Mr. Francis.

THE END OF THE SECOND BOOKE.

The Third Booke.

NOW fals it out in order to declare,
    What time is best to Angle in aright;
    And when the chiefe and fittest seasons are
Wherein the fish are most dispos'd to bite,
What winde doth make, and which againe doth marre
The Anglers sport, wherein he takes delight,
    And how he may with pleasure best aspire,
    Vnto the wished end of his desire.

For there are times in which they will not bite,
But doe forbeare and from their food refraine,
And dayes there are wherein they more delight
To labour for the same and bite amaine;
So, he that can those seasons finde aright
Shall not repent his trauell spent in vaine,
    To walke a mile or two amidst the fields,
    Reaping the fruit this harmlesse pleasure yeelds.

And as a ship in safe and quiet roade,
Vnder some hill or harbour doth abide,
With all her freight, her tackling and her load,
Attending still the winde and wished tide,
Which when it serues, no longer makes aboad
But forth into the watry deepe doth slide,
   And through the waues deuides her fairest way
   Vnto the place where she intends to stay.

So must the Angler be prouided still,
Of diuers tooles, and sundry baytes in store ;
And all things else pertaining to his skill,
Which he shall get and lay vp long before,
Then when the weather frameth to his will,
Hee may be well appointed euermore,
   To take fit time when it is offered euer,
   For time in one estate abideth neuer.

The qualities of an Angler.

NOW, ere I farther goe, it shall behoue
   To shew what gifts and qualities of
     minde
   Belongs to him that doth this pas
     time loue ;
And what the vertues are of euery kinde
Without the which it were in vaine to proue,
Or to expect the pleasure he should finde,
   No more then he that hauing store of meate
   Hath lost all lust and appetite to eate.

For what auailes to Brooke or Lake to goe,
With handsome Rods and Hookes of diuers sort,
Well twisted Lines and many trinkets moe,
To finde the Fish within their watry fort,
If that the minde be not contended so,
But wants those gifts that should the rest support,
   And make his pleasure to his thoughts agree,
   With these therefore he must endued be.

The first is Faith, not wauering and vnstable,
But such as had that holy Patriarch old,
That to the highest was so acceptable
As his increase and of spring manifolde.
Exceeded far the starres innumerable,
So must he still a firme persuasion holde,
   That where as waters, brookes, and lakes are
     found,
   There store of Fish without all doubt abound.

For nature that hath made no emptie thing,
But all her workes doth well and nisely frame,
Hath fild each Brooke, each Riuer, Lake and
  Spring,
With creatures, apt to liue amidst the same;
Euen as the earth, the ayre, and seas doe bring
Forth Beasts, and Birds of sundry sort and name,
   And giuen them shape ability and sence,
   To liue and dwell therein without offence.

The second gift and qualitie is Hope,
The Anchor-holde of euery hard desire;
That hauing of the day so large a scope,
He shall in time to wished hap aspire,
And ere the Sunne hath left the heauenly cope
Obtaine the sport and game he doth desire,
    And that the Fish though sometimes slow to bite,
    Will recompence delay with more delight.

The third is Loue, and liking to the game,
And to his friend and neighbour dwelling by :
For greedy pleasure not to spoile the same,
Nor of his Fish some portion to deny
To any that are sicklie, weake, or lame,
But rather with his Line and angle try
    In Pond or Brooke, to doe what in him lyes
    To take such store for them as may suffice.

Then followeth Patience, that the furious flame
Of Choller cooles, and Passion puts to flight,
As doth a skilfull rider breake and tame
The Courser wilde, and teach him tread aright :
So patience doth the minde dispose and frame
To take mishaps in worth and count them light,
    As losse of Fish, Line, Hooke, or Lead, or all.
    Or other chance that often may befall.

The fift good guift is low Humilitie,
As when a Lyon coucheth for his pray.

So must he stoope or kneele vpon his knee,
To saue his line or put the weedes away,
Or lye along sometime if neede there be
For any let or chance that happen may,
   And not to scorne to take a little paine,
   To serue his turne his pleasure to obtaine.

The sixt is painefull strength and courage good,
The greatest to incounter in the Brooke,
If that he happen in his angry mood,
To snatch your bayte, and beare away your
    Hooke:
With wary skill to rule him in the flood,
Vntil more quiet, tame, and milde he looke.
   And all aduentures constantly to beare,
   That may betide without mistrust or feare.

Next vnto this is Liberalitie,
Feeding them oft with full and plenteous hand,
Of all the rest a needfull qualitie,
To draw them neere the place where you wil
    stand,
Like to the ancient hospitalitie,
That sometime dwelt in Albions fertile land,
   But now is sent away into exile,
   Beyond the bounds of Isabellas Ile.

The eight is knowledge how to finde the way
To make them bite when they are dull and slow
And what doth let the same and breedes delay,
And euery like impediment to know,

That keepes them from their foode and wanted
  pray,
Within the streame, or standing waters low,
    And with experience skilfully to proue
    All other faults to mend or to remoue.

The ninth is placabillitie of minde,
Contented with a reasonable dish,
Yea though sometimes no sport at all he finde,
Or that the weather proue not to his wish.
The tenth is thankes to that god, of each kinde,
To net and bayt doth send both foule and Fish,
    And still reserue inough in secret store,
    To please the rich, and to relieue the poore.

Th' eleauenth good guift and hardest to indure,
Is fasting long from all superfluous fare,
Vnto the which he must himselfe inure,
By exercise and vse of dyet spare,
And with the liquor of the waters pure,
Acquaint himselfe if he cannot forbeare,
    And neuer on his greedy belly thinke,
    From rising Sunne vntill a low he sineke.

The twelth and last of all is memory,
Remembring well before he setteth out,
Each needfull thing that he must occupy,
And not to stand of any want in doubt,
Or leaue something behinde forgetfully:
When he hath walkt the fields and brokes about,

It were a griefe backe to returne againe,
For things forgot that should his sport maintaine.

Here then you see what kinde of quallities,
An Angler should indued be with all,
Besides his skill and other properties,
To serue his turne, as to his lot doth fall :
But now what season for this exercise
The fittest is and which doth serue but small,
   My Muse vouchsafe some little ayd to lend,
   To bring this also to the wished end.

Season and time not to Angle.

FIRST if the weather be to dry and hot,
   And scalds with scorching heate the lowly plaine
As if that youthfull Phaeton had got,
   The guiding of his fathers carre againe,
Or that it seem'd Apollo had forgot
His lightfoote steedes to rule with stedfast raine,
   It is not good with any line or Hooke
   To Angle then in riuer, pond, or brooke.

Or when cold Boreas with his frosty beard,
Lookes out from vnderneath the lesser beare
And makes the weary trauailer afeard
To see the valleys couered euery where

With Ice and Snow, that late so greene appear'd,
The waters stand as if of steele they weare:
  And hoary frosts doe hange on euery bough,
  Where freshest leaues of summer late did grow.

So neither if Don Æolus lets goe
His blustring windes out of the hollow deepe,*
Where he their strife and strugling to and fro
With triple forke doth still in order keepe,
They rushing forth doe rage with tempests so,
As if they would the world togither sweepe
  And ruffling so with sturdy blasts they blow,
  That tree and house they sometimes ouerthrow.

Besides when shepheards and the swaines prepare
Vnto the brookes with all their flockes of sheepe,
To wash their fleeces and to make them faire,
In euery poole and running water deepe,
The sauour of the wooll doth so impaire
The pleasant streames,† and plunging that they
    keepe,
  As if that Lethe-floud ran euery where,
  Or bitter Doris intermingled were.

---

* The stronger the wind blows, so you may abide it and guide your tools, and the colder the summer days are, the better will they bite, and the closer [*nearer*] shall you come to them.—W. L.

† I rather think the kades and other filth that fall from sheep do so glut the fish, that they will not take any artificial bait. The same is the reason of the flood, washing down worms, flies, frog-clocks, &c.—W. L.

Or when land flouds through long and sudden
    raine,
Discending from the hills and higher ground,
The sand and mud the christall streames doe
    staine,
And make them rise aboue their wonted bound,
To ouer flow the fields and neighbour plaine,
The fruitfull soyle, and meadowes faire are
    drownd
  The husbandman doth luse his grasse and hay,
  The bankes their trees, and bridges borne away.

So when the leaues begin to fall apace,
And bough and braunch are naked to be seene,
While nature doth her former worke deface,
Vnclothing bush, and trees, of summers greene,
Whose scattered spoiles lye thicke in euery place,
As sands on shore or starres the poles betweene,
  And top and bottome of the riuers fill,
  To Angle then I also thinke it ill.*

---

* Most of us are aware of the old rhyme :—

> When the wind blows from the west,
> It blows the hook to the fish's nest;
> When the wind blows from the south,
> It blows the hook to the fish's mouth,
> When from the north and east it blows,
> Seldom the angler fishing goes.

My dear friends and pupils, don't believe it : if you possess a copy of this bit of ancient doggerel, let it be

All windes are hurtfull if too hard they blow,
The worst of all is that out of the East,
Whose nature makes the Fish to biting slow,
And lets the pastime most of all the rest,

---

anything but a rule for your conduct. You may have
sport in all winds and in all weathers, or you may not;
as long as the wind is not too heavy and is *up-stream*,
be sure that you have the best wind that can blow for
fly-fishing, though it is less favourable for the float. I
have had some of the best days I ever had in my life
with a north or east wind, and some of the worst
with a south or west one. Some will say, choose a
cloudy day with a wind here or there, and some a
rainy day with the wind nowhere; some say, never
fish in thundery weather, whereas I have caught fish
again and again, and known them caught, in all
possible sorts of weather, even with the thunder
cracking all round—nay, directly overhead. I do not
believe there is any rule whatever that can be relied
upon. I have had first-rate sport in a snow-storm
ere now, and two years ago a friend and myself took
eighty-four brace of trout averaging about three-
quarters of a pound each, in three days, the weather
being pleasantly varied by north easters, sleet, and hail
storms. The influences which cause fish to feed, or
the reverse, are as much a mystery to us as they were
to our forefathers. Fishes' appetites are doubtless
somewhat like our own—they feed best when they
are hungry, and when they can do so with the least
fear. Fish feed at some time in the twenty-four
hours, and be sure if they are not rising it is because
there are no flies to tempt them. They are not
starving by way of amusement, rely upon it, but have
‘metal more attractive’ down below in the shape of

> The next that comes from countries clad with snow,
> And Articq pole is not offensiue least,

---

grubs, worms, larvæ, &c. No one perhaps would willingly select a bright hot day, with no wind and a low water, yet I have at times had excellent, nay, the best of sport even, on such days. And few would choose a steely bright day with a cutting easterly wind, and little or no fly on the water; but on two such days running I once, in Derbyshire, killed in the brightest possible water forty-six brace of capital trout each day. I could have killed more on the second day, but did not care to carry them, and I have often had good sport on similar days; some of the best days I have had were on bitterly cold days with a north-east wind, and little or no fly on; and some of the worst on warm cloudy days with a south and south-west wind and plenty of fly. Upon the other hand, how often will the angler go out upon a day which he would have picked out from the whole year, had he the choice, and do little or nothing. There are some days—nice, brisk, cloudy days—with a steady breeze, and not too much fly, and the water in good order, which the angler may pretty well count upon as being good days, and be seldom deceived, though he may sometimes, even then; but as to picking out a day when he can be sure that the fish will not feed, it is beyond his skill. He may of course chance to be right and he may chance to be wrong, and the longer he is a fisherman the more he will discover that he does not know how a day may turn out until he turns out his creel at night. It not unfrequently happens that some very slight and unex-

The southern winde is counted best of all,
Then, that which riseth where the sunne doth
 fall.*

Best times and seasons to Angle.

BVT if the weather, steadfast be and
 cleare,†
 Or ouercast with clouds, so it be dry,
 And that no signe nor token there
 appeare,
Of threatning storme through all the empty skie,
But that the ayre is calme and voide of feare,
Of ruffling windes or raging tempests hie,
 Or that with milde and gentle gale they blow,
 Then is it good vnto the brooke to goe,

---

pected change will take place, some new fly will begin to hatch out, or some other insect will put in an appearance, which sets all the fish feeding suddenly, and will thus afford him an hour or two's capital sport, turning a bad day into a good one. My advice to the young angler is: always carry your macintosh, be patient and persevering, and leave the weather to take care of itself.—Francis *On Angling*, pp. 163-5.

* I find no difference of winds; except too cold or too hot : which is not the wind, but the season.—W. L.

† Clear cannot be good, by reason of the offensive sight.—W. L.

And when the flouds are fall'n and past away,
And carried haue the dregges into the deepe,
And that the waters waxe more thin and gray,
And leaue their bankes aboue them high and steepe,
The milder streame of colour like to whay,
Within his bounds his wonted course doth keepe,
 And that the wind is south or else by-West,
 To Angle then is time and seasons best.

When faire Aurora rising early shewes*
Her blushing face beyond the Easterne hils,
And dyes the heauenly vault with purple hewes,
That far abroad the world with brightness fils,
The Meadowes greene are hoare with siluer dewes,
That on the earth the sable night distills,
 And chanting birds with merry notes bewray,
 The neere approaching of the cheare full day.

Then let him goe to Riuer, Brooke, or Lake,
That loues the sport, where store of Fish abound,
And through the pleasant fields his iourney make,
Amid'st sweet Pastures, Meadowes fresh and sound,

---

* The morning can no way be good because the fish have been at relief all the night, as all other wild creatures : and in the day they rest or sport. In the evening is the fittest. Then hunger begins to bite.—W. L.

Where he may best his choice of pastime take,
While swift Hyperion runnes his circle round;
   And as the place shall to his liking proue,
   There still remaine or further else remoue.

To know each fishes haunt.

NOW that the Angler may the better know,
   Where he may finde each Fish he doth require,
   Since some delight in waters still and slow,
And some doe loue the mud and slimy mire;
Some others where the streame doth swifter flow,
Some stony ground, and grauell some desire,
   Here shall he learne how euery sort doe seeke,
   To haunt the Layre that doth his nature like.

Carpe, Eele, and Tench, doe loue a muddie ground,
Eeles vnder stones or hollow rootes doe lye;
The Tench among thicke weedes is soonest found,
The fearefull Carpe into the deepe doth flie,
Bream, Chub and Pike, where clay and sand abound,
Pike loues great pooles, and places full of frie:
   The Chub delights in streame or shadie tree,
   And tender Breame in broadest lake to be.

The Salmon swift the Riuers sweet doth like,
Where largest streames into the Sea are led :
The spotted Trout the smaller Brookes doth seeke,
And in the deepest hole there hides his head :*
The prickled Pearch in euery hollow creeke,
Hard by the banke, and sandy shoare is fed.
 Pearch, Trout, and Salmon loue cleere waters all,
 Greene weedy rockes, and stony grauell small.

So doth the Bulhead, Goodgion, and the Loache,
Who most in shallow Brookes delight to be,
The Ruffe, the Dace, the Barbill and the Roach,
Grauell and sand doe loue in lesse degree,
But to the deepe and shade doe more approach
And ouerhead some couert loue to see,
 Of spreading Poplar, Oake, or Willow greene,
 Where vnderneath they lurke for beeing seene.

The mighty Luce great waters haunts alway,
And in the stillest place thereof doth lye,
Saue when he raungeth foorth to seeke his pray,
And swift among the feereful fish doth flye,
The dainty Humber loues the marley clay,
And cleerest streames of champion countrie hye,
 And in the chiefest pooles thereof doth rest,
 Where he is soonest found and taken best.

---

* The trout lies in the deep; but feeds in the stream, under a bush, bray, foam, &c.—W. L.

The Chauender amidst the waters fayre,
In swiftest streames doth most himselfe bestow,
The Shad and Tweat doe rather like the laire,
Of brackish waues, where it doth ebbe and flow,
And thither also doth the flocke repaire,
And flat vpon the bottom lyeth low,
   The Peele, the Mullet, and the Suant good
   Doe like the same, and therein seeke their food.

But here experience doth my skill exceed,
Since diuers Countries diuers Riuers haue ;
And diuers Riuers change of waters breed,
And change of waters sundry Fish doth craue,
And sundry Fish in diuers places feede,
As best doth like them in the liquid waue,
   So that by vse and practise may be knowne,
   More then by art or skill can well be showne.

So then it shall be needlesse to declare,
What sundry kindes there lie in secret store,
And where they doe resort, and what they are,
That may be still discovered more and more :
Let him that list no paine nor trauell spare,
To seeke them out, as I have done before,
   And then it shall not discontent his minde,
   New choice of place, and change of game to find.

The best houres of the day to Angle.

FROM first appearing of the rising sunne,
    Till nine of clocke low vnder water best
    The fish will bite, and then from nine
        to noone,
    From noone to four they doe refraine
        and rest,
From foure againe till Phœbus swift hath runne
His daily course and setteth in the West:
    But at the flie they vse to bite,
    All summer long from nine till it be night.

Now least the Angler leaue his Tooles behinde,
For lacke of heed or haste of his desire,
And so inforced with vnwilling minde
Must leaue his game and backe againe retire,
Such things to fetch as there he cannot finde
To serue his turne when neede shall most require,
    Here shall he haue to helpe his memory,
    A lesson short of euery wants supply.

Light Rod to strike, long line to reach with all,
Strong hooke to hold the fish he haps to hit,
Spare Lines and Hookes, what euer chance doe fall,
Baites quicke and dead to bring them to the bit.
Fine Lead and Quils, with Corks both great and small,
Knife, File and thred, and little Basket fit,

Plummets to sound the depth of clay and sand,
With Pole and net to bring them safe to land.

And now we are arriued at the last,
In wished harbour where we meane to rest;*

---

* Under the heading of "Certain Observations forgotten," William Lauson adds:—
Chevan and Chub are one.

The { Shotrell, 1 year; Pickerel, 2 year; Pike, 3 year; Luce, 4 year } are one.

The Summer—May, June and July—are fittest for Angling.

Fish are the fattest in July.

Fish commonly spawn at Michael's tide [29th September]. After spawning; they be kipper, and out of season.

They thrust up little brooks to spawn. The Trout and Salmon will have lying on their backs.

All the summer time, great fish go downwards to deeps.

Bar netting and night hooking; where you love Angling.

When you are angling at the ground: your line must be no longer than your rod.

He that is more greedy of fish than sport: let him have three or four angles fitted and baited: and laid in several pools. You shall sometimes have them all sped at once.

If you go forth in or immediately after a shower, and take the water in the first rising; and fish in the stream at the ground with a red worm: you may

And make an end of this our journey past:
Here then in quiet roade I thinke it best
We strike our sailes and stedfast Anchor cast,
For now the Sunne low setteth in the West,
   And yee Boat Swaines a merry Carroll sing,
   To him that safely did vs hither bring.

---

load yourself, if there be store. Thus may any botcher kill fish.

For want of a pannier : spit your fish by the gills on a small wicker or such like.

I use a pouch of parchment, with many several places to put my hooks and lines in.

I use a rod of two parts, to join in the midst when I come to the river : with two pins and a little hemp waxed. Thus the pins join it, and the hemp fastens it firmly.

A whale bone made round, no bigger than a wheat straw at the top; yields well, and strikes well.

Let your rod be without knots. They are dangerous for breaking, and bouts are troublesome.

Keep your rod neither too dry nor too moist ; lest they grow brittle or rotten.

When you angle in [a time of] drought, wet your rod. It will not break so soon.

You shall hardly get a rod of one piece, but either crooked or top heavy or unequally grown.

Enterprise no man's ground without leave. Break no man's hedge to his loss.

Pray to GOD with your heart to bless your lawful exercise.*

---

* Dame Juliana Berners gives the same excellent advice.

Wouldst thou catch Fish?
Then here's thy wish;
Take this receipt,
To annoynt thy Baite.

THOU that desir'st to fish with Line and Hooke,
Be it in poole, in Riuer, or in Brooke,
To blisse thy baite, and make the Fish to bite:
Loe, here's a meanes,* if thou can'st hit it right.

---

* I have heard much of an ointment that will presently cause any fish to bite; but I could never attain the knowledge thereof. The nearest in mine opinion—except this *Probatum*—is the oil of an Osprey, which is called *Aquila Marina*, the Sea Eagle. She is of body near the bigness of a goose; one of her feet is webbed to swim withal, the other hath talons to catch fish. It seems the fish come up to her: for she cannot dive. Some likelihood there is also in a paste made of *Cocculus Indiæ*, *Assafœtida*, Honey, and Wheat-flour. But I never tried them. Therefore I cannot prescribe.

That which kills the oak, I conjecture to be Ivy, till I change my mind. This excellent receipt: divers anglers can tell you where you may buy it.—W. L.

Take Gum of life, fine beate and laid in soake
In Oyle, well drawne from that which kils the Oake,
Fish where thou wilt, thou shalt haue sport thy fill,
When twenty faile, thou shalt be sure to kill.
       PROBATUM.

Its perfect and good,
If well vnderstood;
Else not to be tolde
For siluer or golde.
      G. K.

APPENDICES.

APPENDIX I.

Perch Fishing.

The perch is usually described as a bold biting fish, and so he may be where he is not much fished for, or where perch are over-plentiful and small, or when, like other fish, they have a hungry day; but if by the above character it be meant that good perch are deficient in wariness, then I contradict it. Where they are at all fished—and my remarks apply to rivers and lakes where they are well and regularly fished for—there are few fish more capricious or careful in biting than large perch; small ones may often be taken in any quantity, but not so when they gain experience. I have known places haunted by numbers of good perch—perch of from a pound and a half to three pounds in weight—and yet, season after season, there are seldom more than one or two of them caught, and these nearly always at the starvation part of the year, *i.e.* after the heavy winter floods, when the small fish are all driven up the brooks, and the perch are driven into the few still eddies that exist. Here, while the river is tearing down outside in a spate, from one to two hundred, and sometimes more, perch will often be congregated in a space of some ten or twenty square yards, perhaps. After these fish have battled with the frosts of winter, on short rations for weeks, what chance has a minnow among such a host, or what chance even a hundred minnows? No wonder, then, that you pull them up two or three at a time, one for each minnow; the only wonder is that they do not, in their eagerness, swallow the plummet of your paternoster in its descent, by mistake. In truth and faith, January and February are deadly months for poor Perchy. Cabined, cribbed, confined in a black hole of an eddy, they are pulled out not in braces, dozens, or even scores, but often to the tune of hundreds. I have seen and helped to catch ten dozen and over out of one hole, and have heard of twice ten dozen being taken. But catch Master Perch on a fine summer's day, in this way, if you can. Often have I, through the crystal clear water, watched the proceedings of a dozen perch at the worm or a minnow on my hook, some twelve or thirteen feet below. How they come up to it with all sail set, their fins extended, their spines erect, as if they meant to devour it without hesitation! and how they pause when they do come up to it, and swim gently round it, as if a worm or a minnow were an article of vertu, which required the nicest taste, and the consideration of a connoisseur to appreciate it properly. At length one of the boldest, taking hold of the extreme tip of the tail as timidly as a bashful young gentleman takes hold of the tip of his partner's finger when he leads her to the festive quadrille, will give it a shake. Now, if you are curious, watch your float; see how it bobs down, after a fashion that would make you think the perch must not only have swallowed the bait, but half digested it; whereas, in fact, they cannot make up their minds about it. Is

it a safe investment or is it not? Is it real old
Chelsea or only a modern imitation? And then
comes an aldermanic perch, of nigh two pounds, a
warm liveryman of the Fishmonger's Company, a
regular turtle-fed lord mayor elect, with his cheeks
blown up, his eyes staring out of his head, his fins all
bristling with magisterial importance. 'Now then,
what is this case! Ha, hum! a worm, eh? yes.
Found hanging about the streets with no ascertainable
occupation, and without any home, eh? Ha! bad
case—very bad! a mysterious and vagrom character,
evidently. Take him away, some of you, and lock
him up—very suspicious indeed, very much so.' And
so his lordship, having taken a half turn, and a brief
survey of the wretched trembling culprit, who with
policeman hook stuck into him, Alderman Perch
looking at him angrily and hungrily, and limbo gaping
at him from Mr. Alderman's stomach, is drawn up as
useless and thrown on one side ; while, with a fan of
his tail, the alderman scuttles off to a fresh case, and
all his little people scuttle off after him, save, perhaps,
one unhappy little devil who won't take warning.
Anyone who wishes to see this portrayed, should look
at poor Arthur Smith's lithograph of Rolfe's picture,
called 'The Committee of Taste.' It is a grand bit of
expression, and the combination of greediness, inquis-
itiveness, pomposity, and funk, in the picture, is
perfectly delicious. But to my angling.

There are various ways of catching perch. The
first, and most common, is with the live minnow, or,
if minnow cannot be had, any other small fish, or fry
of gudgeon, dace, or roach, will do ; but these should
only be used when the angler has no other alternative,
as, although the perch is infinitely the more desirable
and valuable fish, fry should not be wasted. There
are four ways of using a minnow, all of which will

take perch : viz. with a float and either one or two hooks, or a paternoster with two or three, with a loose line and roving minnow, or by spinning.

With the float, the lowest hook (if two are used) should be two or three inches off the bottom, and the next one should hang between mid-water and the bottom. The best way of baiting the minnow is to pass the hook tenderly and carefully through the gristle of the upper lip; some choose the back fin. but a minnow so hooked neither lives so long nor moves so freely as when hooked by the lip. When a perch takes the float down, do not strike directly, as the tackle used for this fishing being usually fine, it is as well to make sure of him; for, in spite of anything that some sceptical anglers may say to the contrary, the scratching and losing of one or two perch does most indubitably very often—I won't say always, because there may be exceptions, but does very often —drive the shoal away. I have noticed it scores of times, and have heard many good and experienced anglers verify the fact. Therefore rather give him a little time, and even let him leave the bait, or cut it off, in preference to being too hasty and scratching him.

The paternoster is simply a gut line, a yard or four feet long, with hooks about a foot apart, and weighted at the end with a bullet or pear-shaped plummet. Some anglers use three hooks and some two, a necessity which is more often regulated by the depth of the water to be fished. But the lowest hook, unless the bottom is unusually foul, should be almost on the ground, as it is the habit of the minnows to strike up toward the surface in their efforts to escape, just as it is the habit of all fish when pursued by an enemy; fear causes them to seek the surface, and even to jump out of the water. Therefore if the minnow be not kept down, it will be much above the head of such perch as are lying at the bottom; and, if the water be at all coloured (as is best for perch-fishing), this will not only be a fault, but a great one; whereas if the hook be kept close down to the lead, it will catch two or three fish against either of the other hook's one. The second hook should be fixed nine inches above, and must hang clear of the tie of the lower hook. This is the best form of paternoster made.

The localities in which to look for perch vary with the season. Early in the summer the angler will find them in the streams, as in gudgeon-swims, into which they come when the ground is raked or disturbed, and here they often take the angler's gudgeon worm ravenously; indeed, perch occasionally take a worm almost as well, and in some cases even better, than they do the minnow. They are often taken on the ledger, and these are frequently the best fish too. Some time since I was fishing with a friend on the Thames; we were dace-fishing, with the float line; he had a paternoster out on his side of the boat for perch; I had a ledger on my side for barbel; I had at least a dozen bites, and caught two or three nice perch, while he never got a touch, with a choice minnow and a small gudgeon not four or five yards off, and the perch were feeding all round us. As the summer advances, the perch seek the deeper and stronger streams, the quiet eddies and deep holes near piles, lock-gates, piers of bridges, corners of weirs, and by heavy weed banks. At this time they are well fed and cautious, and will try the angler's skill to make a good dish of them. As the season advances, and the winter floods sweep down, they all draw into the great eddies, or still corners, particularly after a sharp frost, and here they will be found in great numbers; and when the water is a little coloured, they may be taken in from three to seven or eight feet of water, or deeper, in any quantity, as they are then hungry, though in good condition. As March comes on, they get heavy in spawn, when they should not be disturbed. By the middle of April they get amongst the weeds, rushes, or fibrous roots of trees, in still back-waters, and here they deposit their spawn in long ropy glutinous masses. It is astonishing what a vast number of eggs the female perch will v' id; they are very small, and about the size and of th[,] appearance of little seed pearls. Perch spawn about the end of April, and get into fair season again by the end of June.

Perch may often be caught with a spinning minnow, but it is not a very common method of angling for them, though the best fish are usually so caught; and I have known good execution done in lakes by spinning, either with a minnow (real or artificial) or a spoon. Indeed, I almost think, from my experience, that I am justified in saying that they take a spoon better than almost any other spinning bait; but I have found them prefer the triangular spinner made of spoon metal (commonly called the 'otter') to the regular spoon, the only reason I can give for it being that it spins better and more evenly than the spoon, which wobbles a good deal; and though this is liked by pike, and not always objected to by trout (particularly lake trout), it would seem that it is not a strong recommendation to perch.

A handful or two of gentles or broken worms will be found useful as ground-bait, when float-fishing with worms. But whatever you do, do not take your wife's or sister's gold-fish globe out with a muslin cover on it, and a stock of lively minnows inside, under the supposition that the perch will rub their noses against the glass, like cats at a dairy window, according to the old superstition.

APPENDIX II.

Pike Fishing.

The most sportsmanlike way of fishing for pike is certainly by spinning, which is thus practised. The angler takes a small fish (gudgeon, dace, or bleak are preferable—if these cannot be obtained, he may use any other small fish which he can get); he then hooks the fish on to his line by a certain arrangement of hooks called a flight or set, so that by communicating a crook to the body or tail it may, when drawn through the water, revolve rapidly on the screw principle. In order to permit the bait so to revolve without twisting the line, a tackle called a trace is used. This is about four or five feet long, and consists of a few strands of stout salmon gut, or of gut twisted, or even of gimp, linked together with a couple of swivels at intervals, about eighteen inches apart, a third swivel being sometimes used, to connect this part of the tackle with the running or reel line; a good large loop being left at the other end of the trace to loop the flight of hooks on, or for the purpose of changing them at pleasure. The trace should not be less than from a yard to four feet long, and not more than five, or it will be found awkward in casting. Between the swivels the lead or sinker is to be fastened. In ponds, where the weeds come very near the surface, a sinker may be dispensed with, and the bait be allowed to run almost along the surface of the water. In this instance the simpler the arrangement of hooks, and the fewer there are of them, the better.

According to the depth or swiftness of the water or stream to be fished, so should the weight of the lead be; and this is a point to which considerable attention should be paid, as it is sometimes necessary to fish shallow. Of the two, I prefer to fish deep, as the less distance a pike has to come after the bait the better, for pike will not always come to the top of the water after the bait, even if they see it; and when they do come, they will see the deception so much more easily that, if they are not tolerably hungry, they will often refuse the bait. This is especially the case with good fish. Many a time have I, when fishing rather high, seen a good ten or a dozen-pounder come up with a dash at the bait and after following it for a yard or two, turn tail and leave it, when, probably, had I been fishing deep, he would just have put his nose out of the weed and snapped my bait. But there is a great advantage in fishing high when the fish are hungry. You cover so much more ground—that is to say, the fish can see the bait so much farther off. Of course, if the fish are well on the feed, and are ranging for food, it will matter little whether the angler fishes high or low, as within any reasonable distance his bait will be seen laterally, and probably run at. Whether it be taken or no, however, of course depends on the opinion the fish forms of it on nearer inspection. One point the angler should bear in mind, viz. that he cannot (provided the bait turns round fairly, so as to display itself well and hide the hooks) spin too slowly: and if he *over*-weights his line, in order to keep it clear of the weeds at the bottom, he will be obliged to spin so quickly, or to draw the bait along so rapidly, that he will not give the pike a fair chance of biting. Too swift spinning is a great fault and it is, indeed, too common a fault in these fast days. The angler likes to be always throwing. 'Swish!'—out goes thirty or fourty yards of line. 'There's a throw Smith, my boy!' He likes to see his bait spin like a humming top. 'Look at that, Smith, my boy! can you make a bait spin like that?' Possibly Smith cannot make a bait spin in that wonderful way, and cannot throw above twenty or thirty yards of line; but somehow Smith, with a short line, runs more fish than our fast friend. It has been the popular myth that a bait travelling at railway pace, and spinning like one long line of silver, is the correct thing, because it imitates a fish in an agony of terror. This argument is sheer nonsense, as fish do not conduct themselves like dancing dervishes or ballet-masters, and perform pirouettes when in a fright. They run away and turn perhaps, from side to side, as the swimmer does, to gain increased power by concentrating every effort now to one point and then, as a relief, to the other. The long, slow wobble of a badly-spinning bait is much more like the *real* thing, no doubt, but it is necessary to make the bait turn somewhat rapidly in order that the pike may not have too much uninterrupted inspection of the eight or ten hooks that encumber one side of the lure, and in order to present the silver side, constantly changing and flashing in the light, to attract the attention of the fish, which a badly-spinning bait will not do; and it is to be borne in mind, that unless the bait spins very well indeed when drawn rapidly through the water, it will, when drawn only moderately slowly (as is preferable), hardly spin at all; therefore it is desirable that the bait should spin well.

The best kind of line for spinning, unless the angler be fishing with Nottingham tackle, or casting from the reel, is slack plaited silk dressed. In choosing the line, see that it be neither too fine nor too bulky. If it be too fine it will be constantly kinking in throwing, and it will not stand the requisite amount of wear and tear attendant on jack-fishing. If it be too bulky it does not go so freely through the rings, and much shortens the cast, besides being too visible to the fish.

If very heavy baits be required and large fish be expected, a stouter line must of course be used. Select a line that is neither too dry nor too sticky as regards the dressing. If it be too dry the dressing on the line cracks in places, and the line becomes more like a land-measuring chain than a fishing-line; and if it be soft and sticky it is a perpetual nuisance in casting, causing endless kinking, and the dressing very soon wears off. It should be fifty or sixty yards long—not that so much will be often required in fishing, but when used well at one end it can be turned end for end with advantage, and answers all the purposes of a new line.

The rod used in spinning for jack should be from twelve to fourteen or fifteen feet in length, with sufficient of spring in it to cast a bait well and yet with good substance to stand the strain and plunges of heavy fish should weeds intervene. Some anglers prefer the rod made of cane; but if it be made of cane, the only kind that should be used for it is bamboo, the other canes having hardly sufficient substance in them. Other persons prefer it made of solid wood, and of all woods greenheart is the best, with a good splinter of the same for the top. That is the rod I prefer. But, whichever may be adopted, the rod should be ringed with good-sized stout upright rings, to allow the line to run through them with perfect freedom.

APPENDIX III

A Select List of Books relating to Angling.

A.

Ancient Classics which allude to Angling.

1. The "Halieutica" of Oppian.
2. The "Mosella," an Idyll of Ausonius.
3. "De Animalium Natura," of Ælian.
4. Poetae Latini Minores. (Several verses in Vol. I. Paris Edition 1824.)
5. Theocritus. (Idyll 21.)
6. The "Geoponika," Book 20, generally attributed to Constantine VII.
7. St. Ambrose, in his "Hexaemeron," Book V.

B.

Bibliographies of Angling Literature.

1. A Catalogue of Books on Angling, by Sir Henry Ellis, in Vol. II. of "The British Biographer," 1812.
2. Pickering's "Bibliotheca Piscatoria," 1835.
3. A List of Books on Fishing, added by Dr. Bethune to his Edition of "The Complete Angler," 1847.
4. A Bibliographical Catalogue of Books on Angling, by Russel Smith, 1856.
5. The New Bibliotheca Piscatoria, by Thomas Westwood, 1861.
6. Bibliotheca Icthyologica et Piscatoria, by D. M. Bosgoed, Harlem, 1874.
7. Angling Literature in England, by Osmund Lambert, 1881.

C.

English Books on Angling.

1. "A Treatyse of Fysshynge with an Angle," by Juliana Berners, 1496.
2. "The Secrets of Angling," by J(ohn) D(ennys), 1613.
3. "Barker's Delight," by Thomas Barker, 1651.
4. "The Compleat Angler," by Isaac Walton, 1653.
5. "The Contemplative and Practical Angler," appended to Franck's "Northern Memoirs," 1694.
6. "Salmonia," by Sir Humphrey Davy, 1828.
7. "Maxims and Hints for an Angler," by Richard Penn, 1833.
8. "A Handbook of Angling," by Ephemera, 1853.
9. "Fly-Fisher's Entomology," by Ronalds, 1847.
10. Stewart's "Practical Angler." 1861.
11. Francis "On Angling," 1876.
12. "Fishing," by Cholmondeley-Pennell, 1885.
13. "The Angler and the Loop Rod," by D. Webster, 1885.*

---

* The list of books here given is only intended as a hint to the angler WHAT to READ: if he wishes to form a COMPLETE Angling Library, I refer him to the contents of Mr. Lambert's book, mentioned above, and the other Bibliographies of Angling Literature.

Finis.

Printed by E. & G. Goldsmid, Edinburgh.

www.ingramcontent.com/pod-product-compliance
Lightning Source LLC
Chambersburg PA
CBHW030405170426
43202CB00010B/1504